The CAMPING COOKBOOK

Annie Bell spent several years as a food writer for *Vogue*, then as a food writer on the *Independent*. She is currently principal food writer on the *Mail on Sunday's YOU magazine*, and is a contributor to *Country Living* and *Waitrose Kitchen*. She was winner of the Guild of Food Writers' Journalist of the Year award in 2003. Her previous books include *Evergreen, Living and Eating, In My Kitchen, Gorgeous Cakes, Gorgeous Desserts, Gorgeous Vegetables, Gorgeous Christmas* and *Soup Glorious Soup*.

The CAMPING COOKBOOK

by ANNIE BELL

PHOTOGRAPHY BY JONATHAN BELL

Kyle Books

Kyle Books
an imprint of Kyle Cathie Limited
www.kylebooks.com
Distributed by National Book Network
4501 Forbes Blvd. Suite 200
Lanham, MD 20706
(800) 462-6420

First published in Great Britain in 2010 by
Kyle Cathie Limited
www.kylecathie.com

ISBN 978-1- 906868-25-3

The Library of Congress Control Number: 2011920342

10 9 8 7 6 5 4 3 2 1

Design: Georgia Vaux
Photography: Jonathan Bell
Editor: Vicky Orchard
Copy editor: Annie Lee
Americanizer: Megan Schmidt
Food and props stylist: Annie Bell
Production: Gemma John

Extract on page 84 from *Swallows and Amazons* by Arthur Ransome, published by Jonathan Cape. Reprinted by permission of The Random House Group Ltd. Extract on pages 72–3 from *Five Go Off in a Caravan* (1946) by Enid Blyton © Chorion Rights Limited, a Chorion Company. All rights reserved.

Color reproduction by Sang Choy in Singapore
Printed and bound by Toppan Leefung Printing Ltd
in China

CONTENTS

WHY CAMP AT ALL?

To anyone studying human behavior from afar, it must seem puzzling that people should choose to abandon the comfort of their own home to sleep under a tent (or in an RV, boat or trailer), which might be seen as trading down. So why do we do it, and during our vacations at that?

We can arrive at this answer from any number of directions, given the tribal element of camping. One of the ironies is that while a camping trip may be fanned by a desire to escape, you only regroup once you have arrived. If you cannot define yourself in terms of "wilderness camper," "glamper," "hiker" or "sail camper," to mention just a handful of types, you still have the opportunity to join any number of camping preferences that will ensure you are surrounded by like-minded people at the other end. So I can but offer a small glimpse into my own incentives or reasons why I find the notion attractive, although I am sure they will be shared by many, whatever subcategory of the genre you belong to.

Socially, camping was popularized in the early twentieth century, and increases in popularity year after year. So much so that I cannot help but link it to the rise in our sophisticated electronic lives, which veer ever further from the basic pleasures of nature. Camping is a way of reconnecting, of stepping back from the constant onslaught of screens and technology and taking a long, deep breath. The place it occupies, or offers to occupy, within ourselves becomes ever more poignant.

When I started writing this book, one of the great surprises was discovering how many of my close friends go camping, not necessarily for weeks at a time, but for a night here and there. It has become a recreational weekend activity for many, largely because it is so accessible. When preparing for the first time out, it is a simple case of keeping an eye on the weather forecast, dreaming of an adventure in some not-too-distant place, and setting off in whatever direction you choose, depending on whether you are seeking the sea, mountains or rolling fields.

When talking to a neighbor the other day, he recounted the first time he took his son camping. They pitched a tent in the woods, got up in the middle of the night and set off with a pair of night-vision binoculars to watch owls. His son was instantly hooked, and the many camping trips that ensued remain precious memories of their time together. It catapulted me back to my own first experience, not so very far from home, when my brothers and I would pitch a tent in the back yard and sleep there. I don't recall ever lasting much beyond five o'clock in the morning before the lure of the warmth inside the patio doors proved too great to resist, but it was long enough to experience half of the day normally spent tucked in our beds. The way the air cools as soon as the sun sets, seeing the moon rise and the stars come to life, even the damp air of the very early morning that cuts through to your joints as you get older, can be a pleasure.

Camping doesn't have to happen far from home; despite the slightly competitive edge, you don't have to scale a mountain and throw your pop-up tent into a slate-lined crater where no man has ever camped before in order to qualify. It's not about brownie points, there is just as much pleasure to be had from pitching a tent in a neighboring farmer's field or the nearby woods and living wild for a night over the weekend as from making a huge trip. And if you have a large yard, there is plenty of fun to be had from setting up camp out of sight from the house and cooking and sleeping there. Nor does it have to involve physical deprivation – should you feel you have to have a bath at night before going to sleep, it isn't going to lessen the experience.

But this brings me full circle to the main reason I'm into camping at all, which, at the risk of creating yet another tribe, is dinner. One of the aspects I most appreciate is the opportunity camping provides to reconnect with food in a way that reflects the surroundings. The way we cook and eat in our everyday lives has become every bit as sophisticated as our electronic existence. Food has become hugely complicated – if you buy take-out, be it pizza, pasta, or Chinese, just count the number of ingredients it contains. And equally, when we are cooking at home, the style and fashion has become heavily-influenced by restaurant culture, and has to compete with that sophistication. To cook and serve the kind of food you might have at home over the weekend would seem out of place on a camping trip, but equally, the wonderfully simple and rustic fare that is so good eaten outdoors might seem lacking at a dinner party.

Rarely do we get the opportunity to touch base with such simple food, true to the ingredients and stripped of all unnecessary frills and preparation. This is what inspires the chapters that follow. The honesty of the experience – using the simple means available – is something to be cherished. That and its recipient counterpart, appetite, which takes on new meaning in the great outdoors, are worth enjoying in trade for all the discomfort in the world.

OUR CONVERSION

It all began with my husband's birthday. The year being celebrated should really have left us thinking more about giving up rather than embarking on a camping trip. But while considering the possible ways of celebrating, we settled on a boat trip along a stretch of river that held happy memories for us both, with a picnic somewhere along the way. In the midst of searching for a boat rental, however, Jonnie accidentally (or so he says) clicked on the "boats for sale" icon on a marina's website, and within the time it took to say "Captain Bell," we were the proud owners of a sailboat called *Winkle*.

It had a cabin, mind you, and that afforded us membership into the great fraternity of travelers who cook for pleasure with no fixed address, without any walls to speak of, let alone such conveniences as running water, who are known as "campers." Although we had yet to become "fully paid-up" members, as hardcore campers are inclined to look on those with

boats and camper vans as "off-peak members," we had arrived. Full enrollment would come sooner than either of us could have imagined.

Winkle, as you might gather from her name, is on the small side. In fact she is to yachts what Beagles are to Great Danes, and it took all but one very uncomfortable night and one marital tiff to realize that you would have to be a) Very Small, and b) Very Young to actually sleep on her. We were neither.

Unlike house descriptions, which can be stretched, when boats, tents, and RVs advertise "sleeps two," what they really mean is "sleeps one-and-a-half." Together with our son we were three. Also, with boats, unlike houses, there is no expanding up or down. We had to figure out a new way to work with our circumstances.

The next logical step was to acquire a tent, which did make us "fully paid-up" members of the camping fraternity. I was particularly excited to discover that we even belonged to a rare tribe called "sail campers," who travel from one destination to another by boat and camp when they get there. I suspect this term is more readily applied toward seriously adventurous types who go white-water rafting along the Amazon rather than puttering up and down some half-mile of our local river, but we were happy all the same. We began to feel that we belonged.

As the summer unfolded and we joyfully recounted our weekend trips to friends and family, we were amazed at how many seemed to be enjoying the occasional camping trip too. Another side to life opened up as we found ourselves planning get-togethers in unlikely places – the opportunity for new adventure seemed endless.

Though it wasn't the easiest of learning curves. The first being that there was almost always a tremendous gap between the trip you thought you were going on and the one that actually took place. As one friend of mine put it, "Just go assuming that you are going to have an awful time and then you'll be pleasantly surprised." The first few trips were just short of disaster, and I am sure there will be many more of those to come. However I have learned to expect the unexpected, put each situation in perspective, and take deep breaths. It is an essential set of tools to possess while living in the great outdoors, tools never utilized more than when you are cooking dinner.

The simplicity of cooking over an open fire outdoors, with the most basic set of utensils, touches a primitive nerve, one that is always there eager for the chance to be rekindled. A day spent gathering ingredients, whether foraging in the wilderness or scouring unfamiliar local markets, followed by an evening around the fire watching the light fade and taking in the scent of food grilling and simmering as the air starts to acquire its night-time chill, is pure magic. So there you have it, a Damascene conversion. And if it can happen to me, it can happen to anyone.

GUIDE TO A GUIDE

As a culinary writer I can perhaps be forgiven for thinking that the most important aspect of camping is eating. Cooking outdoors, and the challenges it brings, are among the most enjoyable aspects of any trip. We do, however, need to begin by throwing away the rule book, and that of course creates the requisite need for a new one. Gone are the conveniences of running water, upon which so much of our cooking at home depends, the shelter of walls, the oven and food processor controlled by the touch of a button. In their place comes unpredictability, and the need to cook with our gut. And that is the fun, connecting with ingredients in a way that is missing from our everyday lives. But with the right equipment and the right approach, we have meals that will settle in our memory for years to come as some of the best we have ever eaten.

The great challenge when camping for the first time is preparing for the trip. Somehow, we have to try to condense the essentials of our home kitchen into a fraction of the space. There is plenty that we can live without, and the trick is to pare it down to the very minimum. There are some brilliant ergonomic designs geared towards campers, although not everything I recommend will be found in Outdoor/Camping stores (see pages 12–24) – a great deal of it is just well-designed everyday equipment. The growing pressure on space in our own homes makes a lot of domestic equipment just as practical on a camping trip.

When we cook at home we have a choice between the range and the oven, so replicating these heat sources is the first consideration. If you are traveling very light, your needs will be met by a backpacking stove such as a Trangia, the design of which holds me in awe. The entire kit unravels like a Russian doll and takes up the space of a medium saucepan. Within it you have your heat source, a couple of saucepans, a frying pan and a kettle. If weight and space are less of an issue you may want to turn to a portable gas stove. However for most people the addition of a portable grill will best provide those precious evenings spent relaxing in the open, drawing in the scent of food on the barbecue. If it is possible to rustle up an open fire, you have the option of cooking on a tripod, or grilling over the open fire. Because there are different methods for cooking outdoors, all the recipes here are geared for one of two general cooking mediums, single burner or grill, which is indicated by an icon beside each recipe.

Having packed up your kitchen, the next consideration is how to squeeze the contents of your pantry into the small space that remains. If we have to take just one little part of the world with us on our trip, then let that be the Mediterranean. The scents and flavors of its shores capture everything that is alluring about cooking outdoors. The Traveling Pantry that follows is the Mediterranean in your pocket.

Bringing it all together are the essentials of olive oil, lemon juice and garlic. So step number one is to combine these ingredients into convenient forms before you leave: this is the Camping Marinade (see page 27), a golden key. On its own you need nothing more for meat and fish destined for the grill, but with the addition of a few succinct spice blends you broaden your horizons. These spices can either be prepared at home before you go, or you can order them online (see pages 28–9). A second key, albeit smaller, is Camping Glaze (see page 28), a blend of honey and mustard, which you can use to coat meat and fish and also combine with the Camping Marinade to create a delicious salad dressing.

From here the recipe chapters take you from dawn until dusk, starting with a hearty Cowboy Brunch to banish the morning chill and set you up for the day's activities ahead. Then taking you right through to the end of the day are recipes for making a comforting mug of cocoa with cookies for dunking, before you retire to your sleeping bag. In between, children can be packed off on a picnic adventure with an array of treats; there is a chapter on fast appetizers and little eats, should you make new friends or have old ones visiting; and the dinner-time chapters revolve around one-pot dishes, with lots of recommendations for portable grills, including more ambitious dishes like butterflied shoulder of lamb and a whole salmon steamed between long wild grasses. There is also a chapter on cakes to make and take with you, some of which can be used to create more elaborate desserts. And of course, there are all the camping favorites like bananas baked in their peel and roasted marshmallows.

At the heart of all of this is the essential consideration: a lack of water. All the recipes are designed to keep your need for it to a minimum, not only in the preparation of food but also in the cleaning up. A plastic basin and a bit of cold water can very quickly erase the magic of the meal that's just been eaten, so I promise that at the very most you might have one pan to clean. Nor do the recipes require measuring cups, unnecessary items to lug along. Instead measurements are given as a relaxed "handful," "tablespoon," "mug," and the like.

Writing this in the middle of winter, I can't wait for warmer weather to go camping again, and start planning the next feast. Although I may not wait until summer comes around. You just might find me spending a weekend cooking out in my back yard, playing camping. It's hard to resist.

ESSENTIAL KIT

Before shopping for camping equipment for the first time, I glanced around my kitchen – all those treasured items. And suddenly that old adage "everything but the kitchen sink" acquired new meaning.

The question here is when does "essential" become "non essential"? It will have everything to do with how you normally cook at home and how much you feel you are able to sacrifice, a decision that will be widely subjective. A good peppermill, for instance, is non-negotiable in my book. Camping stores may sell those little push-button mills, brilliant in design but without character in action. The satisfying sensation and scent of black peppercorns grinding at a twist of the wrist, and the scrunch of flaky sea salt between my fingers, are rituals I cannot imagine foregoing before putting food onto the grill or into the pot.

Equally you may have some large, unwieldy, heavy pot that cooks in a particular way and gives you a huge amount of pleasure to use outdoors. So pack it up and squeeze it in. Unless you're hiking, in which case your choice of equipment will be necessarily austere, there is a good chance you will be travelling by car, and just might be able to make room. Much of what follows isn't available from camping stores or even designed with campers in mind, it's just well-designed and ergonomic.

I reckon I can fit the whole caboodle into a reasonably-sized wooden crate (which doubles as a prep table once unpacked), with a separate small box containing a "traveling pantry," a grill and stove, and a couple of coolers. Each recipe that follows lists below it the basics of what will be required to cook it, without listing the obvious like a cutting board, utensils and plates to eat from.

Cooking

GRILL

There are some brilliant designs for portable grills out there, and they seem to get more compact by the year. But there is a big difference between being ergonomic and cooking like a dream. And just because they fold away into next to nothing doesn't mean they necessarily perform well.

If you are used to cooking on a kettle grill it is difficult to conceive of going back to an open one, where the heat is difficult to control and the wind whips up the ash and fans the flames. There are various options here, but Weber's iconic charcoal kettle grill, designed by George Stephen in 1951 in Chicago, remains a brilliant piece of design. Later it became known as the "Sputnik" after its resemblance to the Russian satellite.

Stephen fashioned his prototype from a shipping buoy, by cutting it in half, sticking legs in the base, cutting vents in the top and bottom to control the heat, and using the top as a lid. All kettle grills today are based on these principles. The lid not only reduces flare-ups but creates an oven so that the food cooks inside at the same time as charring the outside. It also serves to keep out the rain and wind, making it the best possible all-weather option.

Travel kettle grill

The "Smokey Joe," a miniature Weber kettle grill, is a little bulkier than other portable types, but if you have the space it's a guarantee of great results. The handle clips over the lid so you can carry it without any ash falling out, or even move it from place to place once it's lit. You can also employ the indirect method, in which the coals are piled up on either side, for cooking slightly larger cuts and meat and fish on the bone that take longer than 20 minutes, which is about the limit for grilling over a fierce heat without burning.

Weber's "Go-Anywhere," which is shaped like a box, works on the same system. www.weber.com

Cobb Grill

The Cobb is an ingenious traveling grill. First dreamt up in rural Africa as a green and fuel-efficient way of cooking, it was originally fuelled by dry corn cobs, hence its name. It finds more and more fans every year. Its great features include the traveling case, which means you can pack it up and go while it is still hot; the speed at which it heats up; and that it can roast a whole chicken and potatoes (a meal which, for many of us, is a holy grail whether camping or at home), in addition to smaller cuts.

It's a great system if you're away for a night or a weekend and have access to a dishwasher at the end. The bowl contains a moat that collects the fat from the food as it grills, which isn't something you want to be tackling with a plastic bowl in the middle of nowhere. So for hardcore campers with limited facilities I'd recommend a traditional barbecue such as a small Weber, in which the fat burns off the grill as the food cooks and it can be cleaned with a wire brush or piece of crumpled foil at the end – no water required. www.cobbq.com or www.cobbamerica.com

Chimney starter

Not essential but a piece of equipment that makes lighting a grill exceptionally easy – a hollow metal tube with holes around the outside, which is filled with charcoal and lit with newspaper from below. Within 30–40 minutes the charcoal is furnace-hot. www.weber.com

Wire brush

There's no scrubbing of pots and pans with a grill, just a quick rub down once it's cooled down. Using a wire brush is ideal, although crumpled foil can be used in its absence.

STOVE

Trangia is the original stormproof expedition stove, first produced in the 1920s, and today it is regulation issue for the Swedish military. It opens out like a Russian doll, the size of a cake pan, and it contains two small saucepans and a frying pan that doubles as a lid, a kettle and a burner. Most other camping stoves of the same ilk are copies of this one. More recently they have introduced anodized ultra-light aluminium versions that

provide a non-stick surface. These come with the option of fuel or gas. www.amazon.com

Alternatively, the slightly bulkier option is a gas stove. The larger of these will have two rings, and it's worth buying one with a windshield. For a family of four away for a week who are likely to be cooking a fair deal this is likely to be more practical. www.REI.com

Propane or fuel

Given the many challenges of cooking outdoors, it is a complete joy to be able to command the heat for your food at the touch of a button. The most portable single-ring systems such as the Trangia will have a small propane attachment, while the larger camping gas stoves will come with a bottle. You get a longer burn time with propane than you would with alcohol or gasoline, so if you have slow or one-pot cooking in mind, it is a more practical option.

However, a small alcohol burner such as the Trangia version provides the most portable solution to a single ring, with the advantage that you have a ready supply of fuel in a comparatively small bottle. The downsides are the relatively brief cooking time and the lack of control over the heat, which can be set at either simmer or boil but rarely in between, so for more sophisticated cooking this can be an issue. But if all you want is to boil water, fry some bacon in the morning, or heat up some soup, then it's all you need.

TRIPOD AND DUTCH OVEN See page 21.

Storage

COOLERS

Even the most efficient cooler chests and bags only work to keep food at the temperature in which it is put into the box, as opposed to chilling it down as a refrigerator would. Every time you open up that lid, you are allowing a little warm air to get in.

Days one and two of camping are relatively easy on this front. If you chill your food down well before leaving, a good cooler chest should keep it at that temperature. It also works well to freeze things like sausages and grilling meats – small cuts should have thawed by the evening, while anything larger will last overnight, acting as an ice-pack in the process. But otherwise, shopping is something to look upon as a daily activity, a pleasure when it involves seeking out a local market, farmstand or little fish shop in a seaside village.

For the purposes of traveling light, there are some great soft-sided cooler bags, which are the ones I favor when sailing down the river in our little boat – they can be squeezed into lockers, and fold up into nothing once they are empty.

THERMOS

It's worth taking a thermos of hot water – even if not for drinks, it'll come in handy for washing up. Or fill it with lovely ice water for drinking. The Thermos Work Series Vacuum Insulated Beverage Bottle keeps 40 ounces of liquid either hot or cold for 24 hours. www.thermos.com

WATER CARRIER

The ideal is a plastic carrier that will pour while lying on the ground, otherwise you need a table to place it on. There are many versions available, typically 5 gallon. Another solution is an enamel pitcher that you can decant into. www.amazon.com

PLASTIC STORAGE CONTAINERS

Hard to imagine camping without a set of plastic storage containers. These have come a long way since the early days of Tupperware, which has been superseded by containers with wings on the lid that clip down on to the base. Lock & Lock are the original of their type and are 100 percent airtight and spillproof. Perfect for anything messy that needs to go into the cooler, as well as for marinating foods – you can shake them without any risk of leakage, which does away with a lot of messy mixing. A stackable set of about seven should meet all your requirements, including the Camping Marinade and Camping Glaze. The corners of square ones are good for pouring. www.amazon.com and www.bedbathandbeyond.com

STACKABLE BOWLS

A set of colorful plastic preparation bowls travel light and will double as serving dishes. Joseph Joseph make excellent sets, the larger of which also include a sieve, a colander and either measuring spoons or a lemon squeezer. www.josephjoseph.com. We also love the reusable plastic bowls from Preserve, which are inexpensive, made of 100 percent recycled plastic and are BPA and melamine free. www.preserveproducts.com

TRAVEL CONTAINERS

For just a few days away we only need small quantities of essentials for the pantry. I find the ideal containers are lightweight aluminium screw-top tins (about 3 ounces), which are non-breakable and perfect for spice mixes, sugar and salt. These are available from cosmetic suppliers, who also have small aluminium bottles that are good for decanting liquids and oils. Be sure the containers are listed as "food grade." www.specialtybottle.com

Preparation

CUTTING BOARD
Worth every inch of space, this will double as a work surface in challenging situations when you don't have a table. A folding one makes good sense. www.josephjoseph.com.
Cork cutting boards are a good lightweight option and they float, if that is a consideration. www.greenfeet.com

KNIVES
One small and one large sharp knife
Hard to get away with less. A chef's traveling knife roll will accomodate not only these but a can opener and corkscrew too. www.cheftools.com

Serrated knife
Great for tomatoes and salami, and less likely to slip than other knives if you are cooking anywhere rough. This also doubles as a travel-size bread knife for baguettes, bagels and small loaves.

Pocket knife
For one night away and light cooking you may be able to get away with a single pocket knife without any additional ones. If it has attachments such as a bottle opener, corkscrew and scissors, all the better.

Chopper
This piece of non-essential gadgetry is a trip back in time. These choppers are still around and in better form than ever – the stainless-steel version is good and sturdy and does away with the need for knives when chopping herbs, garlic and onions. They're tear-free too. OXO's "Good Grips" version is particularly easy to work with. www.oxo.com

Other Implements

A potato peeler
Or not...you may be happy with small baked potatoes or new ones cooked in their skins.
A wooden spoon or two
A can opener
A corkscrew
A ladle if you are cooking soup or stews
Tongs

Pots and pans

If you have a camping stove such as the Trangia, you may already be outfitted with a few basic pans and a kettle. The advantage here is that they are lightweight and take up almost no room. The disadvantage is that they are more likely to burn food, and they tend to be on the small side. As an alternative to these, whatever you have in the kitchen will do. At the very least I would take a good-sized non-stick pan.

LARGE POT OR SAUCEPAN
This is essential to one-pot dishes. If you are cooking on a sturdy camping stove, there is no reason not to lug your favorite cast iron dutch oven with you. But my favorite large dedicated camping pot, which covers all the bases, is a Trangia "Billy" or Cook Pot (such as the 4.5 liter version). Made of lightweight aluminium, it also has a handle for hanging, so you can use it for tripod cooking as well. www.nwbackpack.com. Another option if you plan on cooking on a tripod over an open fire is the Lodge system (see Dutch oven, right).

DUTCH OVEN

While hefty, these big cast iron pots really come into their own when you are either slow or one-pot cooking. If you buy one with a handle designed to hang on a tripod you'll have the wherewithal for cooking over an open fire. The cast iron manufacturer Lodge has been catering to itincrant cooks since 1896. A cast iron skillet and Dutch oven were normally the only pieces of cookware early American families possessed. These pots have small feet on them, which is worth bearing in mind if you also want to use one on a gas ring, as you would need an ordinary cast iron pot for this. Lodge also produces a "lid lifter" for use on the tripod, to keep an eye on the food as it cooks. www.lodgemfg.com

DREAM-POT

I was very skeptical about how useful I would find one of these Australian portable slow cookers, but it only took two or three times of using it to realize just how indispensable it might become. It could have been designed around the Indian-style lunchbox or "tiffin carrier": two saucepans – one very large and one smaller one that fits into the top – will hold two different dishes, perfect for stews or casseroles with rice, for instance. The idea is that you start cooking with these, for perhaps a quarter of the usual cooking time, and then pop them into your Dream-Pot, which has an outer casing that works like a thermos. It clips shut and has a handle for carrying it. The food continues to cook very slowly, and is perfectly cooked and piping hot 2–3 hours later. It cannot overcook, even if you leave it for 7 hours, but would simply require a little reheating at that point. www.dreampot.com.au

FRYING PAN

A good-sized non-stick frying pan is essential. There are now some excellent "green" non-stick pans on the market, such as the "GreenPan," which has a thermalon coating. Almost like enamel, it is in fact ceramic, and we can fry away with a clear conscience that we're not harming the environment or ourselves. www.amazon.com

COLANDER

If you have one of the stackable sets of bowls (see page 18) you are set, but otherwise a plastic collapsible colander folds flat. Most of the recipes are designed to get around the need, but they're useful for washing fresh fruit and vegetables. www.josephjoseph.com

Eating

PLATES

Many houseware departments will have biodegradeable plates, bowls and the like. The Rolls Royce of these, however, are made from bamboo veneer. They are designated for single use, but if it's just a few crumbs they can be wiped down and reused. www.greenfeet.com. Otherwise enamelware remains a classic and practical camping option. www.campmor.com

CUTLERY

Knives, forks and teaspoons can all be obtained in biodegradeable materials, which will save on the washing up. But a teaspoon and tablespoon are essential measuring tools in the recipes that follow.

MUG

An essential measurement in many of the recipes that follow, a little over 1 cup (8 ounces) in capacity. The best kind for camping are enamel or aluminum.

TUMBLERS

We can live without long-stemmed glasses; all they do is fall over. One tumbler suits all.

SKEWERS

Wooden ones that can be burnt at the end of the barbecue are ideal – soak them in water first. But a few metal ones won't take up much space and can take on a little more strain. Flat ones will ensure the food doesn't slip around.

SALT AND PEPPER

Using a peppermill is second nature in the kitchen. I was dreading having to leave my Peugeot mill at home (these are widely-regarded as the best grinding mechanisms), but they also produce an adorable mouse of a mill called the "Bistro" that measures just under 4 inches. (www.chefsresource. com). As for the crunchy salt, bring enough for the trip in a small aluminum or plastic container.

And don't forget

BRIQUETTES
Charcoal briquettes tend to burn more consistently than lumpwood, which can be erratic.

LIGHTERS
There are special long, lighters for grills that are an essential in my book. www.amazon.com

LONG MATCHES

FOIL
In the absence of an oven, foil is endlessly useful for baking food in a package on the grill, as well as for lining a frying pan, for instance when cooking bacon to minimize clean up.

GARBAGE BAGS
A variety of sizes come in handy, but especially small ones.

TENTS
The range of tents available in today's market is vast. From high-tech backpacker tents and designer family tents to high-quality historic wilderness tents the choices can make your head spin. Consider your spacial needs, your portability limitations and your budget. The choices will soon become clear. We find some of the best all-around online camping resources for tents to be Cabela's, Campmor and REI. Traditional canvas tents are available from smaller, specialty manufacturers like Tentsmiths out of New Hampshire and Soul Pad in Texas.

www.cabelas.com
www.campmor.com
www.REI.com
www.tentsmiths.com
www.soulpad.com

TRAVELING PANTRY

A traveling pantry is the golden key. But how daunting, to pare all those different oils and vinegars, bottled sauces, spices and dried herbs down to a desert island collection of essentials. Or, as my husband puts it, "How many types of peppercorn does a girl need?" Answer: seven. On the other hand, it is liberating to discover just how little you really need to create a wonderful range and array of dishes.

Life is made that much easier by honing in on just one flavor palette — and for a life outdoors that has to be the Mediterranean. The intensity of flavor, the color, the sheer panache and relaxation that go hand in hand with the food of Spain, Italy, Greece, the Middle East and North Africa capture so much of what we are seeking when we pack up our camper vans, RV's or load the tents and sleeping bags into the car, idly looking ahead to the moment when we will light the fire and while away the hours gazing into the flames and drawing in the scent of meat or seafood sizzling on the grill.

Bringing it all together, a luscious green olive oil, the sharp tang of fresh lemon juice, the pungency of garlic and a good sea salt. So step one in creating our "traveling pantry" is to combine all these into what will be called Camping Marinade, which takes all of 5 minutes before you go.

Dressed simply with this elixir, lamb chops, chicken pieces, a steak or pork fillet will be divine with a simple green salad and some warmed bread in tow. And it's easy to take it one step further with the addition of a succinct spice blend. Again you don't need anything extensive here: a Moroccan and a Middle Eastern blend will have a myriad of uses.

Allowed to sneak in a couple of extras, a small package of Jerk Seasoning is possibly my favorite barbecue classic. Some Italian Seasoning (a blend of dried basil, oregano, garlic, onion and pepper) can be sprinkled over warm pita bread and drizzled with oil for the simplest of pizza-style breads, scattered over grilled chicken and vegetables, and added to dressed salad greens.

Two more ingredients that I use endlessly at home are honey and Dijon mustard. These can be combined into what will be known as Camping Glaze, which can be used to give chicken, sausages and other proteins a lovely sticky finish on the grill. It can also be mixed with the Camping Marinade to create a glorious salad dressing. A handful of basics in addition are all that you need. You may not want everything that's suggested, but whip up the basic marinade and glaze and you have the foundation for pretty much everything you might want to barbecue or serve as a salad.

Marinade and Glaze

CAMPING MARINADE

Good for a couple of meals for 3–4 people

This marinade is perfect as it stands – you need nothing more to prepare meat or fish for the grill. You can also use it as a building block, by adding herbs such as thyme, oregano or marjoram, rosemary or herbes de Provence.

Or you can add one of the suggested spice blends (see page 29) to whisk you to the shores of Morocco or to the Middle East. Either way, this means you are effectively working with only two ingredients while you are cooking.

⅓ cup lemon juice (2–3 lemons)
½ cup extra virgin olive oil
3 garlic cloves, peeled and crushed into a paste
1 teaspoon sea salt

Combine all the ingredients in an airtight container, such as Lock & Lock (see page 18) and shake before use. Store in a cool place.

CAMPING GLAZE

Good for a couple of meals for 3–4 people

Possibly my all-time favorite glaze, for everything from the skin of roast chicken to an array of sausages. Combine it with the elixir on the previous page and you have a delicious honey mustard salad dressing. It's easy to whip up more of this, should you require, but this is a good amount to start off with.

4 tablespoons Dijon mustard
4 tablespoons country-style honey

Blend the two ingredients in a bowl and store in an airtight container, such as Lock & Lock (see page 18).

Spices

If you are to take just two blends with you, they should be the Middle Eastern and Moroccan blends that are used most extensively in the recipes that follow.

Although there is no need to take these, or the Jerk Seasoning or herbes de Provence, simply blending them with olive oil and using them as a marinade or to coat whatever you are grilling, they promise tantalizingly good results, with scents that will whisk you off to foreign shores and beaches.

By far the easiest route is to order the spices online from World Spice Merchants (www.worldspice.com), who specialize in replicating traditional spice blends. The spice blends are priced in the $2 per ounce range, with two ounces generally equalling ½ cup. They conveniently come in small lightweight bags, an ideal travel size. But below are recipes for making the key blends yourself (herbes de Provence and za'atar are best bought ready-made). You can either grind the spices yourself or use them ready-ground.

MIDDLE EASTERN SPICE BLEND (*KABSA*)

This fiery blend is scented with that Middle Eastern duo – cinnamon and cumin.

1½ teaspoons cayenne pepper
1 teaspoon cinnamon
1½ teaspoons cumin
1 teaspoon black pepper
½ teaspoon nutmeg
½ teaspoon cardamom
¼ teaspoon cloves
½ teaspoon coriander

Note: green cardamom will probably require sifting once ground.

MOROCCAN SPICE BLEND (*LA KAMA*)

Mellow, peppery and sweet – ginger, black peppercorns, turmeric, cinnamon, nutmeg.

2 teaspoons ginger
2 teaspoons black pepper
1 teaspoon turmeric
1 teaspoon cinnamon
½ teaspoon nutmeg

JERK SEASONING

The allspice, thyme and nutmeg make this such a classic combination. It's worth packing this for making jerk chicken alone, but it will be wonderful with any meat or fish.

3 teaspoons onion powder
2 teaspoons black pepper
2 teaspoons dark brown sugar
1 teaspoon allspice
1 teaspoon dried thyme
1 teaspoon dried chili flakes
½ teaspoon ground nutmeg
½ teaspoon cloves

Note: there is no need to grind the thyme or chili flakes here.

A few basics

Extra virgin olive oil
Sea salt
Black pepper
Chili flakes or Tabasco
Sugar
Dark rum

ALL SYSTEMS CAMPING

A minimal investment of time and preparation before you leave home will make a world of difference to the smooth running of any camp kitchen. More than anything it's about taking advantage of constant running water to get the messy little tasks like squeezing lemons and crushing garlic out of the way, hence the all important Camping Marinade, designed to be whipped up at home before you leave.

THINGS TO DO BEFORE YOU GO

Make Camping Marinade and Camping Glaze
(see pages 27–8)
Order or make up spice blends
(see pages 28–9)
Freeze ice packs
Bake a cake (see pages 58–69)

Wash fruit, vegetables and salad leaves
Sharpen knives
Fill thermos
You could also
Make some garlic butter (see page 150)
Prepare some crushed garlic in olive oil

First build your kitchen

Although this would seem to be obvious, as a novice I found it wasn't. The first night we set off "sail camping" in *Winkle*, I was so relieved to reach our destination, and so hungry from the journey, that I got straight into preparing dinner without considering how to make the whole thing work practically. Within no time our campsite took on refugee status. It was impossible to cook in, with the water carrier at one end, a cutting board on the grass somewhere in the distance, and the essential equipment strewn all over the place. So now I know better – that ten minutes of Guide-to-a-Guide organization makes all the difference.

The great essential is water, as you are almost certainly going to have to transport it by hand to wherever you are cooking. So first there's a need for a carrier, and I also like to have a big enamel pitcher and basin that take over the role of a tap and sink. Second is the need for somewhere to chop or prepare food, which is all but impossible at ground level, but also doesn't need to be as high as an actual table either. Our solution is a big old wooden crate that serves to carry the equipment around, and that, once unpacked, can be turned over into a table of sorts. And last, you need a trash can or plastic bag. There is, of course, endless other paraphernalia to organize or pile on, but sort the basics and the rest will fall into place.

A LITTLE KNOW-HOW

Keeping cold

Slim, flat ice packs seem to give the best coverage within a cooler bag or chest, and can be stacked between items. But in their absence, an empty milk carton filled with water and frozen is a good fix. Then, of course, there is the problem of what to do when they have defrosted. Some campsites will have a freezer, but otherwise, at the risk of being a little bold, you could always ask a shop with an ice cream freezer if you can pop your ice-blocks into it to cool down. Most shops with a half-empty freezer will be happy to oblige.

Stoves  = Recipes using stove

COOKING WITH FUEL

There is little in the way of adverse weather conditions that a stormproof camping set will not be able to cope with. But they do call for a little know-how.

Using a fuel burner, you get a burn time of around 25 minutes on high – this is when the small holes at the base are facing the wind and the air is drawn up past the burner, making it heat the food as fast as possible.

By slowing things down you can double the cooking time: either turn the holes at the base away from the wind, or pop the simmer ring on top of the burner, to extinguish the outer edge of the flame. If you do run out of fuel mid-way, remove the pan, place the burner cap over the burner (having removed the rubber ring inside) and, once the flame has gone out give it a minute or two to cool, then fill and relight it.

Another tip, to help with the washing up, is to add 10 per cent water to your fuel, which will reduce the amount of carbon deposits on the pans.

COOKING WITH PROPANE

If anything differs from cooking with gas at home, it is trying to achieve a really low heat, which can be a little hazardous outdoors where the flame so easily blows out. I would set the flame at a minimum of medium, even when trying to cook a dish very gently.

Grills  = Recipes using barbecue

Portable grills, however fantastic, are limited by their size. At home, where we tend to have larger barbecues, we are used to being able to accommodate a large spread on the grill and cook meat, fish and vegetables all at once, whereas a portable grill basically has the capacity of a single ring stove. While it will do well grilling meat or fish for supper, if you want cooked vegetables too you need either a single burner on which to heat a pan, a second portable grill, or to settle for a salad and breads that are quickly warmed at the end.

LIGHTING UP

The ultimate foolproof way of lighting a charcoal grill is a chimney starter (see page 15). Charcoal is piled into an open-ended cylinder, with a couple of pieces of scrunched up newspaper in the base. Light the newspaper and leave it for half an hour or so, standing it on the grill's grate, and you should have red hot coals coated in the desirable film of light gray ash that signifies they are ready for grilling. Carefully dump them under the grate of the grill and you are good to go.

In the absence of one of these, the principle for lighting coals is pretty much the same. Build a pyramid of charcoal, with either lighter cubes or crumpled up newspaper under the pile of briquets and light. Once they are covered in light gray ash (usually about 25 to 30 minutes), spread them out using long-handled tongs. The mistake so often made is to spread them out in the first place – you end up using a box of matches and the coals at the extremes never catch on.

As for log fires, start small using lots of kindling and paper. As it appears to be taking hold, build it up one log at a time. Using small logs is ideal. Remember to set your fire within a good circle of rocks and stones and never on dry grass or ground covered with fallen leaves.

COBB GRILL KNOW-HOW

With a Cobb grill you need a mere eight briquets to produce a wide range of delicious offerings. The grill's unique design allows fat and oil to drain away from the food without touching the briquets. This makes the Cobb grill practically smokeless, while preserving the desired charcoal flavor. The dome keeps the heat even and preserves moisture.

The grill plate effectively sears the meat, so you need to keep turning a whole chicken, for instance. But it produces beautifully tender and succulent results, with little risk of the burning that can take place with other grills. It also allows you to bake small potatoes that again might burn in a hotter grill.

WEBER OR KETTLE GRILL KNOW-HOW

Kettle grills cook in two ways, either by the "direct" heat method, where the coals are spread out in the usual manner, or by the "indirect" heat method, where they are piled at either side, which enables you to cook a larger cut of meat on the bone without worrying about it burning. The cooking times here are on a par with a hot oven at home, which makes life easy, as there is no great adjustment to make.

COWBOY BRUNCH

Being part of the morning as it comes to life, separated only by a sheet of canvas, is one of the great joys of camping – experiencing the light as it changes, the scents, and the way the damp is driven into remission by the sun, if you're lucky. I can almost forgive the unfamiliarity of a sleeping bag that hasn't lost a single opportunity during the night to remind me that I'm not at home, blocking every attempt to achieve the comfort I'm afforded in my usual bed. So it's up at dawn, and by the time the sun has reached the treetops my appetite has kicked in with a long-forgotten lust for the first meal of the day.

The ideal is a proper, big breakfast, with the opportunity to lounge around drinking mugs of strong black coffee, drawing in the smell of bacon and eggs sizzling in the frying pan. These tantilizing aromas will jolt any snoring souls to surface and join you. And what is that craving for toast slathered with unsalted butter and marmalade or apricot jam, something that I normally can live without from one year to the next?

So the idea here is to satisfy this long-lost friend, appetite, and tuck into breakfast in a frenzy of enthusiasm before going off and climbing a mountain or surfing a few waves, returning to base camp mid-afternoon for a scrumptious snack, before settling into the serious business of supper.

TOAST AND JAM

The craving? I suspect it may be a kind of perverse challenge to the elements and circumstances, because, while the simplest of delights, it presents itself to be a challenge without an electric toaster. And if there is one thing likely to drive our passion then surely it is the elusive. But we WILL have toast. So pack a jar of some particularly fine homemade jam – I have a thing about apricot with unsalted butter, but a chunky strawberry or a thick marmalade are all going to seem equally heavenly with that steaming cup of coffee.

SIMPLY TOAST

The quick route to stisfying that craving is to heat a dry frying pan over a medium flame and toast the **bread** for a couple of minutes on each side as you like it.

Equipment Stove, pan

FLAME-GRILLED TOAST

The method here depends on the nature of the bread. Sourdough, for instance, and other country breads that are normally slow to brown in an electric toaster, do best when drizzled with olive oil before grilling, while more delicate varities, such as ordinary sliced white bread, will be fine without the addition of oil.

The time the toast takes will depend on the heat of the grill, but if very hot you should work according to the timing you would expect at home from a toaster – maybe 1–2 minutes each side for more delicate breads, and 2–3 minutes for **sourdough** drizzled with **oil**.

Equipment Grill

SPANISH TOAST

During some time living in Spain, breakfast at a bar around the corner was a cup of industrially strong coffee and a thick baguette-like slab of bread, toasted, drizzled with olive oil and spread with jam. This technique is ideal for campers, obviously, due to the lack of butter.

Simply toast your **bread** in a dry frying pan over medium heat for a couple of minutes per side until golden. Drizzle with **oil**, or do this first if you want something really crispy, then spread with **jam**.

Equipment Stove, pan

CHOCOLATE TOASTIES

For 2 people

Assuming you don't have access to a patisserie, these little pitas hark back to the days before chocolate croissants became our weekend treat, a time when French children would munch on a length of baguette and a stick of chocolate on their way to school.

Heat a frying pan over medium-low heat. Cut open 2 **mini pita breads**, insert a row of **dark chocolate** squares within each. Grill for several minutes each side, until the chocolate has melted.

Equipment Stove, pan

RASPBERRY PANCAKE

For 1 person

This continues to satisfy the desire for warmth and comfort first thing in the morning. Pancakes are easy to make at home and transport with you. I always get very excited by finding wild berries late in the summertime for these tasty pancakes. "Pick-Your-Own" farms and local farmstands will fill in with various berries earlier in the season.

Heat a large non-stick frying pan over medium heat. Spread a tablespoon of **raspberry jam** over half a **pancake**, scatter a handful of **raspberries** on top and close with the other half, gently pressing down on the fruit. Cook for about a minute per side until warmed through.

Equipment Stove, pan, spatula

FRENCH TOAST

For 2 people

Also known as *pain perdu* or "lost bread," the art here lies in caramelizing the edges with a little honey. It's divine, whether you play to its savory side with crispy bacon, or smother it in more honey, maple syrup, or jam. It also makes a fine stand-in for dessert at the end of the day. With this you don't get away scot-free in terms of the cleaning up, but provided your pan is non-stick, a quick wipe with a paper towel should do it.

1 medium egg
$1/3$ mug of milk
1 tablespoon sugar
butter for frying
2 teaspoons honey
2 slices of white bread or brioche

Whisk the egg with the milk and sugar in a shallow bowl. Heat a non-stick frying pan over medium heat, add 2 tablespoons of butter and the honey. Once these are sizzling, dip the bread into the egg and milk mixture and cook both sides until golden and caramelized around the edges. Spoon any gooey pan juices over the top. If you need to do them one at a time, use just a teaspoon of honey for each slice.

Equipment Stove, pan, spatula

BACON SAMMIES

For 2 people

To eat a warm bacon sandwich out of doors on a morning that's slowly coming to life is to restore one's faith in appetite. And here, so as not to detract from any of the magic, there is no pan to wash at the end.

Line a large frying pan with foil, lay 5–6 strips of **bacon** in the pan and cook over medium heat until golden on either side. You may find they don't brown as evenly as usual on their bed of foil, so keep an eye on them and

move them around as necessary. Now slip the foil with the bacon out of the pan, warm a **pita bread**, slice it in half, fill with the bacon, and add some **ketchup or a dash of hot sauce**.

With egg
You can cook a couple of eggs in the rendered bacon fat left on the foil, with an additional drizzle of oil to assist in finishing off the yolk.

Equipment Stove, pan, foil, spatula for egg

KIPPERED HERRING WITH WHOLE WHEAT BREAD

While vacationing off the west coast of Scotland with friends we discovered this traditional, savory breakfast. Under a canopy of blue sky, we made a fire with driftwood on the edge of the dunes, and strung split herring ("kippers") above it from a makeshift contraption that I seem to recall involved a coat-hanger. Then lots of buttered bread, nothing fancy, as nothing fancy goes in part of the world, with shots of whisky and coffee to follow. It was a late breakfast, so we were ravenous as opposed to just hungry, and the sight and smell of the fish grilling were mesmerizing. So this is an ode to Charlie Boxer, author of that memory and fire-builder supreme.

You need a tripod set over an established log fire, or you could rig something up with coat-hangers strung across as mentioned, anything really that provides the ability to hang the fish. Secure these through the tail with some string, suspend them about six inches above the burning embers or logs, and cook until they are glistening with oil and warmed through – ideally they should be dripping. You are not seeking to cook them as such, it is more a question of bringing them back to life. One **herring** will probably do for two people with a relatively light appetite, a whole one each for more serious eaters. Dish them up with lots of **whole wheat bread** spread with **unsalted butter**. Accompany with **whisky** for the brave, and **coffee**.

Equipment Tripod, string

CRISPY DUCK HASH

For 4 people

This falls at the glamorous end of the hash family, employing a tub of duck pâté. If you think how good potatoes roasted or fried in duck or goose fat are, this is passed on here, with the added richness the pâté brings. There is no need to peel your potatoes before cooking them, the skins turn delightfully crispy.

The idea is that you have potatoes for supper the night before and just cook up some extra with brunch in mind. It's good with any kind of pâté, or, for a different twist, corned beef, in which case you'll need a few tablespoons of oil.

1 x 7-ounce tub of duck pâté
2–3 shallots, peeled and finely chopped
8 small waxy potatoes, cooked and sliced
a couple of shakes of Tabasco (optional)

Melt the duck pâté in a large non-stick frying pan over medium heat, then add the shallots and potatoes and cook for about 20 minutes until golden and crispy. Turn them frequently, and season with Tabasco, if desired.

Short order

A little fruit goes so well with duck – place a few halved plums (about 6 halves should do it) into the pan after you've removed the hash, and brown them on both sides.

Equipment Stove, pan, spatula

ALL-IN-ONE FRY-UP

For 4 people

Lay 8 strips of **bacon** over the bottoms of a large non-stick frying pan, or as many as will fit, and cook both sides until a little golden. Over the top scatter 4 small, sliced **cooked potatoes**, add a handful of **sliced button mushrooms** per person. Drizzle with a little **vegetable or olive oil** and add freshly ground **black pepper**. Keep cooking, stirring occcasionally, for 10–20 minutes, until everything is evenly golden and crispy. Make 4 wells in the mixture and break an **egg** into each one. Cook for 2–3 minutes, then turn using a spatula and cook for a moment longer to set the top, leaving the yolk runny.

Equipment Stove, pan, spatula

HUCKLEBERRY FINN FRY-UP

For 4 people

There is a scene in Mark Twain's *The Adventures of Tom Sawyer* where the "pirates" Tom, Joe and Huck go for an early morning dip and return to their camp "wonderfully refreshed, glad-hearted, and ravenous."

"They soon had the camp-fire blazing up again. While Joe was slicing bacon for breakfast, Tom and Huck asked him to hold on a minute; they stepped to a promising nook in the river bank and threw in their lines; almost immediately they had reward. Joe had not had time to get impatient before they were back again with some handsome bass, a couple of sun-perch and a small catfish – provision enough for quite a family. They fried the fish with the bacon and were astonished; for no fish had ever seemed so delicious before. They did not know that the quicker a fresh water fish is on the fire after he is caught the better he is; and they reflected a little upon what a sauce open air sleeping, open air exercise, bathing and a large ingredient of hunger makes, too."

To this end, heat a few tablespoons of **vegetable or olive oil** in a large non-stick frying pan and add a handful of diced, salt-cured pork fat (or bacon) and cook until slightly golden. Add enough **mackerel or other fish fillets** for 4 people skin down in the pan. Season the fish with **black pepper** and continue until you can see they are almost cooked through. Flip them over and continue to cook briefly until the flesh is just firm. Serve with lots of **buttered whole wheat toast** (see pages 39–40).

Equipment Stove, pan, spatula

SCRAMBLED OMELETTE

For 4 people

Halfway between an omelette and scrambled eggs, what the Spanish would call a *revueltos*, this is a delicious vehicle for any number of seasonal ingredients, but here we make it an excuse to indulge in lots of fondue-esque Swiss cheese and runny eggs. A lovely supper with a tomato salad as well as a delicious meal at the start of the day.

Whisk 8 **medium eggs** with some **seasoning** in a bowl, and mix in a couple of handfuls of thinly sliced **fondue-style cheese** – Gruyère, Beaufort, etc. Heat a large non-stick frying pan over medium heat – any higher and the eggs will scramble instantly without the cheese melting. Add a couple tablespoons of **butter** (or **vegetable oil**) and, once the foam subsides, pour in the omelette mixture and cook it, folding it over a few times as it sets on the bottom, until the cheese is clearly melted but the last of the egg is still runny. Dish it up immediately, served with **hot buttered toast** (see pages 39–40).

Equipment Stove or grill, mixing bowl, pan, spatula

COWBOY BEANS ON TOAST

For 4–6 people

If one thing makes food while camping convenient, it's cans. Canned beans and tomatoes provide an endless array of opportunities. If you have one of those choppers (see page 19), it can be usefully employed here to finely chop the onion, garlic, apple and tomatoes. I'd give the beans a rinse too, by refilling the drained cans with fresh water and draining them again.

a few tablespoons of vegetable or olive oil
3 shallots, peeled and finely chopped
1 garlic clove, peeled and finely chopped
½ an apple, peeled and cut into a small dice
1 x 14½ ounce can of chopped tomatoes
2 tomatoes, peeled and finely chopped
2 x 14½ ounce cans of white navy beans
2 teaspoons light brown sugar
1 teaspoon Dijon mustard
a pinch of chili flakes or a few shakes of Tabasco
sea salt
a few handfuls of slivered salami (optional)
baguette slices, toasted
butter to serve

Heat the oil in a large saucepan or casserole over medium heat and add the shallot, garlic and apple and cook until softened, but not browned. Add all the remaining ingredients and simmer, covered, for 15–20 minutes. Add the salami, if using, for the last 5 minutes of cooking. Drop a few slivers of butter in the center of the pot and leave to melt. Serve with buttered toast (see pages 39–40).

Equipment Stove or tripod, saucepan or pot, can opener

HOT SMOKED SALMON ROLLS

A personal favorite, there are two routes to choose from here, one hedonistic and the other slightly less so. In the first you butter your baguette or rolls on the outside as well as the inside before cooking them, to achieve a seriously crisp and buttery crust. The second route is to butter the inside only. For one or two people, rolls will do nicely, whereas for three or more, baguettes will play to a crowd.

Either way fill them with **smoked salmon**, drizzle with a little freshly-squeezed **lemon juice** and top with freshly-ground black pepper.

You then have two options for cooking them: 1.) Heat a pan over medium heat for 5 minutes, wrap the rolls in foil and heat for 4–5 minutes on each side. Or, 2.) Without wrapping the rolls, toast them for a couple of minutes either side on the grate of a hot grill. Pass the napkins around and enjoy.

Equipment Stove, pan and foil or grill

TRAVELING TREATS

This chapter is arguably the cheat in the equation, as all these recipes are designed on a "cook 'n' go" basis, something to whip up before you leave home. Which is not to say that you can't bake cakes on your grill, your stove or with any other ingenious outdoor equipment you are lugging with you, but why go to the trouble? Baking cakes is a messy business, best performed in a controlled oven with lots of running water and a dishwasher on hand. So bake and take seems by far the most practical solution.

Nothing fancy, mind you – rustic times call for rustic cakes. I am the first to immerse myself at home in the art of decoration, but sticky globs of icing have a habit of attracting unwanted insects when camping and can often make their way into places in which you would rather not come across icing, especially after dark. So, with that in mind, here is a collection of unadorned old-fashioned favorites – a good chocolate sponge cake, a cherry loaf, a dense banana cake, oatmeal pancakes, a fudgy jam sandwich shortbread, a ginger cake and some chocolate chip cookies.

The ideal is either something that can be transported wrapped in foil, and cut into squares or fingers, or a loaf cake, which is that much sturdier than a tiered round one. And flapjacks and cookies are ever transportable, good for passing around in the car while you're sitting in a traffic jam or on line waiting for a ferry.

CHOCOLATE CAMPING CAKE

Enough for several days, or 9 big squares

Brownie-like in its charm, and exceptionally gooey,
so the best way to transport it is in its pan.

14 tablespoons unsalted butter, softened
1 cup superfine sugar
3 medium eggs
4 ounces ground almonds
½ cup flour
5 teaspoons cocoa powder, sifted
2 teaspoons baking powder, sifted
2 tablespoons dark rum
½ cup dark chocolate chips

Preheat the oven to 350°F and butter a 9 inch square cake pan. Place the butter, sugar, eggs, ground almonds, flour, cocoa and baking powder in a food processor and blend together, then add the rum. Transfer the mixture to a bowl and fold in two-thirds of the chocolate chips.

Spoon the cake mixture into the greased pan, smoothing out the surface, and scatter the remaining chocolate chips on top. Bake for 30–40 minutes, until it feels firm in the center and a knife inserted comes out clean. Run a knife around the edge of the pan and leave to cool. Wrap foil around the pan to transport, otherwise it can be cut into quarters and stacked with wax paper or plastic in between the layers.

CHERRY TEA LOAF

Makes a good-sized loaf cake

A classically elegant old-fashioned loaf cake. Ideally you want the dark red undyed preserved cherries here, but maraschino or "cocktail" cherries will do fine.

4½ tablespoons unsalted butter, melted and cooled
4 medium eggs
1 cup superfine sugar
1 teaspoon vanilla extract
⅓ cup heavy cream
1 cup flour
1 heaped teaspoon baking powder
3 tablespoons pulp-free orange juice
½ cup preserved cherries
confectioners' sugar for sifting

Preheat the oven to 350°F. Brush the inside of a 9 inch loaf pan with a little of the melted butter. Unless your pan has a non-stick coating, line the bottom with parchment paper. Whisk the eggs and sugar together in a bowl, then add the vanilla extract and cream. Sift the flour and baking powder together and fold in gradually. Finally stir in the rest of the melted butter and the orange juice, and fold in half the cherries. Pour the mixture into the cake pan and scatter the remaining cherries over the top. They will sink as the cake bakes. Bake for 45–50 minutes, until the cake is golden and has risen. The top should feel completely dry and a knife inserted into the center should come out clean. Leave to cool for 10–15 minutes, then run a knife around the edge of the pan, turn the cake out of the pan and leave on a wire rack, the right way up, to cool. Dust with confectioners' sugar. The cake will keep well wrapped in foil or in an airtight container for several days.

TWICE-BAKED BANANA CAKE

Enough for several days, or 9 big squares

This takes its inspiration from London's Flour Power City Bakery's twice-baked banana cake. Made in a brownie pan, it's baked, smothered in Frangipane and then popped back into the oven to give it a lovely, gooey top.

It's really important that your bananas are overripe, with plenty of bruising – no problem for those who tend to overstock the fruit bowl, but otherwise worth planning in advance.

Cake
2 sticks (8 ounces) of unsalted butter, softened
1 cup superfine sugar
3 medium eggs
1¼ cups flour
1 tablespoon baking powder, sifted
4 tablespoons dark rum
1 teaspoon vanilla extract
3 good-sized overripe bananas, peeled and mashed
½ cup raisins

Frangipane
½ cup ground almonds
6 tablespoons unsalted butter, softened
½ cup superfine sugar
1 medium egg, plus 1 egg white

Preheat the oven to 400°F. Butter a 9 inch square baking pan, line the bottom with parchment paper and then butter this too. Cream the butter and sugar together in a food processor, then incorporate the eggs, then the flour and baking powder, and finally the rum and vanilla. Scoop the cake mixture into a large bowl and mix in the bananas and raisins. Transfer the cake mixture to the prepared pan, smoothing the surface, and bake for 40–50 minutes, until the cake is firm and has risen and a knife inserted into the center comes out clean.

Line a baking sheet with a sheet of parchment paper. Run a knife around the edge of the cake, flip it onto the paper, then remove the base paper from the cake itself. Now leave for about 5 minutes to settle while you make the Frangipane.

Process all the ingredients for the Frangipane in a food processor until smooth and creamy. Spread over the surface of the cake (i.e. the upturned base), bringing it almost to the edge; it will trickle down as it bakes. Return the cake to the oven for 15–25 minutes, until lightly golden. Leave to cool, then slip the cake on to a new sheet of parchment paper or foil large enough to wrap around it. Wrap it up – I normally tie it with string, which makes it easy to carry. It should be good for several days. It's also okay to cut into halves or quarters, as it is relatively sturdy, should it prove easier to transport this way. And as always, its best to store in an airtight container.

GINGER CAKE

Makes 8 generous wedges

My son recently came across a copy of what was my favorite cookbook at his age, *The Pooh Cookbook*, with recipes by Katie Stewart, and I couldn't resist making the honey cake I remembered as being especially good. To give the cake an extra bite I've included more warm and spicy ginger, which elevates the cake to new heights for me. Don't worry if it seems to sink a little in the center – many of the best cakes do, and it'll still be perfectly gorgeous. But if this really worries you, bake it in a 9 inch brownie pan for 30–35 minutes instead.

10½ tablespoons unsalted butter
½ cup light brown sugar
¾ cup country-style honey
2 medium eggs
1 cup plain flour
2 teaspoons baking powder
2 teaspoons ground ginger
a pinch of sea salt

Preheat the oven to 350°F, and butter and line the bottom of a 8 inch springform pan with parchment paper. Gently heat the butter, sugar and honey in a small saucepan until melted and leave to cool for about 10 minutes. Beat in the eggs, then sift in the flour, baking powder and ginger. Fold into the mixture and add the salt. Pour into the prepared pan, giving it a couple of sharp taps to bring up any air bubbles, and bake for 35–40 minutes, until a knife inserted into the center comes out clean. Leave to cool, then remove the sides and the parchment paper and either wrap in foil or store in an airtight container. It is a cake that keeps well for several days, getting stickier as it goes.

JAM SANDWICH SHORTBREAD

Makes 8 generous wedges

This is a French speciality from the Northwest Brittany region. A deliciously cakey shortbread-type of cake with a gooey heart of strawberry jam. The secret of its success being the salty butter.

1 cup self-rising flour, sifted
½ cup superfine sugar
½ cup confectioners' sugar, sifted
2 sticks lightly salted butter, diced
5 medium egg yolks
¾ teaspoon vanilla extract
½ cup jam (wild strawberry, raspberry, etc.)
1 egg yolk, blended with 1 teaspoon water

Place the flour, both sugars and the butter in a food processor and pulse until the mixture is crumb-like. Whisk the egg yolks with the vanilla in a bowl, then add to the dry ingredients and process into a soft, sticky dough. Wrap this in plastic wrap and chill for at least a couple of hours.

Preheat the oven to 350°F, and butter a 8 inch springform pan that is at least 2 inches deep. Press half the dough into the pan, laying a sheet of plastic wrap over the top and smoothing it with your fingers, then remove the plastic. Work the jam in a separate bowl to loosen it, and spread this over the surface to within ½ inch of the rim. Roll out the remainder of the dough on a well-floured work surface (it will still be quite sticky) and shape into a circle slightly larger than the cake pan. Lay this on top of the jam and press it into place, cleaning up the edges with your fingers. Liberally paint the surface with the egg wash, and make a lattice pattern using the tines of a fork. Bake for about 45 minutes, until deeply golden, crusty and risen. Run a knife around the edges and leave to cool (it will sink in the middle), then remove the sides of the pan. This cake will keep well for several days in an airtight container. Serve cut into wedges.

CHOCOLATE CHIP COOKIES

Makes 20–25

A small reminder of the comfort of a
home kitchen and a great negotiating
tool to use with rowdy children.

vegetable oil for greasing
1 stick (8 tablespoons) lightly salted butter, diced
⅓ cup superfine sugar
¼ cup light brown sugar
1 medium egg
½ teaspoon vanilla extract
¾ cup flour
1 teaspoon baking powder
¼ cup raisins
5½ ounces dark chocolate (approx. 70% cocoa), chopped

Preheat the oven to 350°F and lightly grease 2 or 3 baking trays with the
oil. Cream the butter and both sugars together in a food processor, then
incorporate the egg and vanilla. Sift the flour and baking powder and
mix in. Transfer the mixture to a large bowl and mix in the raisins and
chopped chocolate. Drop heaping teaspoons of the mixture in mounds onto
the trays, spaced well apart. Bake for 12–15 minutes, until light golden
brown all over but slightly darker around the edges. Loosen the cookies
right away by carefully slipping a spatula underneath, then leave them
to cool – you can transfer them to a wire rack after a few minutes if you
wish. They are at their best the day they are made, but are still delicious
the day after.

DELICIOUSLY CHEWY OATMEAL PANCAKES

Enough for several days

A good no-frills classic pancake, this has two lives, one as a mid-morning snack, and later on it will double as a crumble topping for whatever soft fruits you're warming on the grill (see page 164).

2 sticks lightly salted butter, diced
¾ cup "sugar-in-the-raw"
6 tablespoons maple syrup
1½ cups rolled oats

Preheat the oven to 350°F. Gently melt the butter with the sugar and syrup in a medium-sized saucepan over medium heat. Stir in the rolled oats. Pour the mixture into a 9 inch square pan or one that's equivalent in size, pressing it down, and bake for 20–25 minutes. Leave to cool and then cut into squares or fingers. Transport wrapped in foil or in an airtight container.

PICNIC DELIGHTS

I know what we'll do this hols! We'll hire a caravan and go off in it by ourselves. Do let's! Oh, do let's!

God, what fun. I was a Blyton junkie as a child, and could happily consume a book a day between breakfast and lunch – for which I count myself lucky, as in my husband's household Blyton novellas were forbidden. Even though she is no longer the middle-class bête noire that she once was, I find it ironic that Enid Blyton is possibly best remembered for her fine food writing. Rarely do you hear her praised for her erudite passages about smugglers and secret tunnels, but get any seasoned Blyton reader on to the subject of "those picnics" and they mist over with nostalgia at the thought of hard-boiled eggs dipped in salt, cake and raspberry sauce and the gallons of ginger beer that washed it all down.

In *Five Go Off in a Caravan*, she doesn't disappoint. There is feast after feast after feast, until you get to Chapter 11, "Fun at the Circus Camp," which kicks off with a gluttonous orgy, with Anne clearing up the breakfast things while Dick goes off to the farm to stock up for the next meal. The farmer's wife shows him "two big baskets full of delicious food. Slices of ham I've cured myself," "and a pot of brawn I've made. And some fresh lettuces and radishes I pulled myself this morning early. And some more tomatoes."

"'How gorgeous!' said Dick, eyeing the food in delight. 'What's in the other basket?'

'Eggs, butter, milk, and a tin of shortbread I've baked.'" She even slips a few homemade sweets into the basket as a parting shot.

While earlier in the book, Anne, who adopts the role of mini-mummy, says, "I've got eggs and tomatoes and potted meat, and plenty of bread, and cake we bought today, and a pound of butter." A pound of butter? They go shopping again the next day, for heaven's sake. I've come to the conclusion, given that this was written in 1946, when post-war rationing was still in place and ingredients like butter, eggs and bacon were scarce, that all these feasts were Blyton's fantasies of the way life should be, after years of wartime hardship.

But they are one of the best aspects of her books: the level of appetite that she conveys, and satisfying it, in a way that is central to life out of doors, is something she captures perfectly. In our coddled, environmentally controlled daily routines, so often we eat because it is time to eat without truly experiencing the hunger that is so enjoyably sated when you are "ravenous." So let us raise a boiled egg to Blyton, dip it in salt and salute the delicious innocence of her picnic delights.

"Nobby went to help Anne. Together they boiled ten eggs hard in the little saucepan. Then Anne made tomato sandwiches with potted meat and got out the cake the farmer's wife had given them. She remembered the raspberry syrup, too – how lovely!

Soon they were all sitting on the rocky ledge which was still warm, watching the sun go down into the lake. It was the most beautiful evening, with the lake as blue as a cornflower and the sky flecked with rosy clouds. They held their hard-boiled eggs in one hand and a piece of bread and butter in the other, munching happily. There was a dish of salt for everyone to dip their eggs into.

'I don't know why, but the meals we have on picnics always taste so much nicer than the ones we have indoors,' said George. 'For instance, even if we had hard-boiled eggs and bread and butter indoors, they wouldn't taste as nice as these.'

'Can everyone eat two eggs?' asked Anne. 'I did two each. And there's plenty of cake – and more sandwiches and some plums we picked this morning.'

'Best meal I've ever had in my life,' said Nobby, and picked up his second egg."

MENU

One of the best parts of this youthful picnic is that there is very, very little to do in the way of preparation. So gather it all together, or even let your children do this, and then send them off with a basket and a blanket to a sandy spot beside the sea or under a shady tree, while you settle down with a good book. Providing them with an ample snack also allows you to bump dinner a little later into the evening, leaving time for a slow-cooked, one-pot dish that requires a couple of hours to simmer.

HARD-BOILED EGGS WITH SALT

I like boiled **eggs** that are slightly runny, therefore I boil them for 6–7 minutes. But if you want them literally "hard-boiled," boil them for 10 minutes. Either way, drain and then refill the pan with cold water. Any leftovers can be turned into Deviled Eggs (see page 89). Serve with a small bowl of **salt**.

Equipment Stove, saucepan

GINGER CAKE WITH RASPBERRY SAUCE

For the raspberry sauce, mix a couple of large handfuls of **raspberries** into 4–5 tablespoons of **raspberry jam** in a jar. Serve this spooned over wedges of **Ginger Cake** (see page 65).

CURRANT BUNS

Spread **currant buns**, or other rolls, with **butter** and quarter. Unsalted butter please (although traveling back through time it would have almost certainly been salted).

CHEESE AND TOMATO SANDWICHES

A satifying and colorful snack sandwich with plenty of room for interpretation. Whether you have cheddar, swiss or mozzarella on hand, the combination with fresh summer tomatoes is delightful. If you happen to have some crisp field greens or peppery arugula on hand, all the better.

Fresh **fruit** and the sparkle of **ginger beer** make the picnic extra special.

UNEXPECTED GUESTS FOR DRINKS

The title of this chapter could have a double entendre, so I should establish that it is the "welcome" kind of guest to whom I refer. The last time we went camping *en famille* on our little sailing boat, *Winkle*, we took the time to reconnoiter along the river where we saught the ideal spot to moor the boat and set up a small tent. We knew from experience that on a beautiful Saturday afternoon these spots tend to get taken long before sundown.

Having settled in and cooked a delicious supper of Roast Lamb with Sweet and Sour Tomato Sauce (see page 127) and a warm pot of Tumbet (see page 103), we attempted a game of mah-jong which we quickly abandoned when we discovered that it is a game best played on a large dining table. We therefore retired to our sleeping bags much earlier than usual. I think we had gotten about two hours of sleep before we heard a loud "ker-splosh" on the water as a squadron of Canadian geese skidded along the surface, grinding to a halt just beside us. I thought birds generally slept at night, but they continued to take off and land, honking loudly, as though practicing some wartime maneuver under the cover of darkness...all night long. Didn't sleep a wink.

Feeling sorry for the wealthy isn't a sentiment that tends to reverberate around family tents, but I did feel quite sorry for the owners of the faux-Georgian mansion that sat on the opposite side of the river. If these "guests" were regulars, you might imagine how the residents of that estate felt on the first night in their beautiful new home. That's one of the good things about camping – you can move on.

In any case, getting back to guests of the "welcome" kind, those old friends game enough to drop by and spend a couple of hours "camping" with you, or the new friends you make – a whole set of new acquaintances made after a week in the wild, sharing the experience together, the camaraderie, is one of true joys of camping. So this chapter is about suggestions for little snacks, whipped up in minutes when such get-togethers come

unexpectedly. These quick and delicious bites are quite good for when you're at home too – why wait to go camping?

SALTED POPCORN

Good for 4–6 people

Popcorn takes up so little space in its unpopped form, and it's a great child bonder – give 'em a big bowl of popcorn and send 'em on their way to sort out the woes of the world together. It's also now officially recognized as a health food, so we should be eating lots and lots of it. And clean up is a snap, you should be left with a completely clean pan that calls for no more than a wipe with a paper towel once it's cooled down.

Heat a drizzle of **vegetable oil** (olive is fine if that's all you have with you) in a medium to large saucepan over very low heat, gently add a single layer of **popcorn** and cover. After about 5 minutes you should hear the occasional pop crescendo into a full-on firework display. So be prepared to hold the lid on tight, giving the pan the occasional shake. Once the popping dies down, remove the pan from the heat, even if you're still getting the occasional pop. Either spoon the popcorn into a plastic bag or leave it in the pan, sprinkle with a little **salt**, tie or cover and give it another good shake to distribute the salt.

Equipment Stove, saucepan

CHIPS "N" DIP

Makes a small container's worth

If you take one of those flimsy plastic containers of dip from the deli counter camping with you, I know from experience the mess that tends to happen when you pop the half-finished container back into the cooler. Better to start from scratch and pack some spreadable Boursin cheese.

Scoop a package of **Boursin cheese** (5.2 ounces) into a bowl and add a few drops of **milk**, blending it with the cheese, until you have a loosened dip. Add **lemon juice** to taste, and serve it up with a big bag of rustic **potato** or **tortilla chips**. **Radishes** or other crudités make a great pairing too.

FETA WITH PISTACHIOS IN HONEY

For 6 people

Feta makes a good traveling companion: its shape, texture and the fact that it comes hermetically sealed all make it a "go-to" in the cooler. But more than that, I love this combination of the salty creamy cheese with the sweetness of honey, and although it's lovely as a little appetizer with a glass of wine before dinner, it will also stand in as a small sweet-savory dessert at the other end of it.

1 x 7-ounce slab of feta cheese
sqeezable honey
a couple of handfuls of pistachios

Combine the pistachios with a couple of tablespoons of honey in a bowl, adding just enough to coat and hold them together. Spread these on top of the feta on a plate, drizzle with a little more honey and dig in. Serve with crackers or crispy toast.

SQUASHED FLY BISCUITS AND CHEESE

In the classic British novel, *Swallows and Amazons*, the children make out like thieves when it comes to dining outdoors, with a birthday picnic basket bursting with goodies:

"...a birthday cake, a huge one with Victoria written in pink sugar on the white icing and two large cherries in the middle. Then there was a cold chicken. Then there was a salad in a big pudding-basin. Then there was an enormous gooseberry tart. Then there was a melon.

Then there were more ordinary stores, a tin of golden syrup, two big pots of marmalade and a great tin of squashed-fly biscuits. Squashed-fly biscuits are those flat biscuits with currants in them, just the thing for explorers."

I'm so glad that Arthur Ransome took the trouble to describe these biscuits, because I was agonizing over how to introduce the subject. A few years after he wrote this book, my husband's parents were on vacation in the South of France, in a rather "grotty villa" according to my mother-in-law, with a great friend who handled the public relations for Aristotle Onassis. The night before they were headed home, a phone call came for their friend informing him that Onassis had just arrived in the harbor on his yacht and thought he might "pop in" for a drink. Needless to say this threw everyone into a complete panic. The pantry was empty, as was the fridge, except for a chunk of Cheddar cheese and a package of Sunshine Raisin biscuits that my mother-in-law had picked up from a corner store on the way back from the beach in anticipation of midnight munchies.

Et voilà, the solution – **squashed fly biscuits** broken into pieces with fine slivers of **Cheddar cheese** on top. Sadly Sunshine Raisin biscuits are no longer produced in the States, but you can find substitutes online.

My mother-in-law has always insisted that these little bites inspired Onassis to invite them onto his yacht for a trip to Portofino.

CHEESE AND HAM PINWHEELS

Makes 6–8 bites

Whipped up in a jiffy, these can also be assembled well ahead of time and heated on the spot. You can warm them on the grill, if you have it going, as well as in a pan on a stove. It takes just a few minutes on each side.

Trim the edges of a **tortilla wrap** to the diameter of the bottom of your pan. Cover the tortilla with thinly sliced **ham**, then lay slices of **sharp Cheddar cheese** in a line about a third of the way in from the edge, then roll it up. Place the wrap in foil, twisting the ends so it is fully sealed.

Heat the pan over low heat for 5 minutes, then warm the wrap for 3–4 minutes on each side. Remove from the foil, slice diagonally into little appetizers, and pass them around.

Equipment Grill, or stove and pan, foil

ZA'ATAR PITAS

Za'atar is a spicy blend of dried thyme, sesame seeds and sumac, a tart red berry that grows wild in the moutains of Lebanon. It's a wonderful, versatile dried seasoning that can be sprinkled over breads and rolls drizzled with oil, and it is worth ordering a small packet if you're buying in your spice blends (see page 28).

Warm some **pita breads**, either on the grill or in a pan on a stove. Slice them open, drizzle some **extra virgin olive oil** over the opened pitas, sprinkle with **za'atar** and serve them either as little pizzettas or slice into thick strips to serve as finger food.

Equipment Grill, or stove and pan

HUMMUS

For 4 people

A can of chickpeas is instantly whisked into a rustic hummus with the two essentials of Camping Marinade and a little Middle Eastern Spice Blend.

Drain a 15-ounce can of **chickpeas** (ideally give them a rinse by refilling the can with water and draining them again). Using a fork, coarsely mash them in a bowl with 4 tablespoons of **Camping Marinade** (see page 27), ½ teaspoon of **Middle Eastern Spice Blend** (see page 29) and a little salt. Don't worry if some chickpeas remain whole, it adds to the charm. Transfer to a small plate, drizzle with a little **extra virgin olive oil** and dust with a little more of the spice blend.

A KIND OF GUACAMOLE

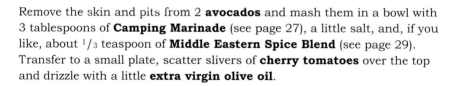

For 4 people

Remove the skin and pits from 2 **avocados** and mash them in a bowl with 3 tablespoons of **Camping Marinade** (see page 27), a little salt, and, if you like, about $^1/_3$ teaspoon of **Middle Eastern Spice Blend** (see page 29). Transfer to a small plate, scatter slivers of **cherry tomatoes** over the top and drizzle with a little **extra virgin olive oil**.

To eat

Serve either of these with tortilla chips or warm pita triangles. Either of these dips can be made more substantial with the addition of black olives, sun-dried tomatoes in oil, or salami.

CRAB PATE

For 6 people

A great cheat – we all know how incredibly expensive crab can be. You can find all kinds of well-priced seafood spreads in specialty markets. Packaged in cans or tubes, they are very portable and make no mess at all. Ikea even sells many Swedish products with prices that can't be beat! Serve with thin slices of baguette, which you can always toast first if you've got the grill going. Crackers are good too.

Blend one 5.3-ounce tube (preferably Abba of Sweden, available online) of prepared **crab pate** in a bowl with a couple squeezes of fresh **lemon juice**, a little **cayenne pepper** and **salt** to taste.

SARDINE PATE

For 4 people

Go for an inexpensive, canned sardine – anything too fancy won't feel at home in the great outdoors. Serve with toast, crackers or bread. It's also good with celery and radishes.

Place 2 generous tablespoons of **softened butter** in a bowl and add 3 cans of **sardine fillets**. Mash together. Blend in 1 tablespoon of **Camping Marinade** (see page 27) and a little **salt**. Transfer to a small plate and sprinkle with fresh, chopped **parsley**.

DEVILED EGGS

For 4 people

However good hard-boiled eggs dipped in salt are, there is a good chance that your children will return from their picnic having finished the Ginger Cake and Raspberry Sauce, but with only one less egg than when they set out. The leftovers can be peeled and dipped into a spicy mayonnaise or for the full retro experience, you could slice them open, spoon the mayo on top and dust with a little more spice. You could also mash any leftover eggs with the spice blend and mayonnaise to make egg salad sandwiches.

Hard-boil 4 **eggs** on the stove (see page 74). Once cooled, peel of the shells. Blend ¼ teaspoon of **Middle Eastern Spice Blend** (see page 29) with 4 tablespoons of **mayonnaise**.

Equipment Stove, saucepan

Other good things for emergencies

Olives: Ideally in resealable plastic bags, which are more convenient than jars and lighter to carry.

Salami: Invest in a whole one for hacking away at with your pocket knife. This is a stable product that doesn't necessarily require refrigeration, the worst-case scenario being that the top slice may dry out.

Salted cashews: They take up less space than chips.

Breadsticks: Ideally artisanal – great for when you don't have fresh bread for dipping.

Cherry tomatoes: Will turn a dip or two, with some bread, into a light supper.

ONE-POTS

One of my most memorable experiences of one-pot cooking was while visiting a market in the Ourika Valley in Morocco early one morning. As we approached the market along a pot-holed mountain road, we could see plumes of smoke gently rising into the air every once and a while. As we got closer we saw that it was, in fact, a line of tagines simmering away over open fires by the side of the road. The vendors would arrive at dawn and, before setting out their wares, would mix up some meat and vegetables with spices and water and leave it to simmer for several hours while they went to work. The results were tantalizing – I longed to join them upon their upturned crates and dip a piece of bread into the soupy juices.

At home, we layer sophistication into our stews by building the flavors in stages, gently softening different vegetables and herbs, searing the meat, reducing the wine and so forth. But look at other cultures and it becomes clear just how good a very basic soup or stew can be. One-pot dishes are by nature the simplest and potentially the most humble of eats. When camping, the most important consideration is perhaps cleaning up, given the lack of water, so it makes sense to plan any meal backwards from the tail end. I have taken us one step further here, inspired by those Moroccan peddlers and abandoning all the usual formalities. The stews, whether taking inspiration from Italy or the wild west, are all "put-it-in-a-pot-and-go." It is surprising how little they lack. I am not suggesting that they are necessarily what you would choose to serve at your next dinner party (although I have done that), but they certainly suit the mood and the occasion.

Due to the simplicity of these dishes, one aspect must be held in the highest regard: the quality of your ingredients. Great components make even the most humble of preparations sing. Shopping at the local markets and farm-stands in the area where you have pitched your tent will guarantee your success at supper time.

NO-CHOP SPAGHETTI PUTTANESCA

For 4 people

As our mainstay pasta dish at home, this remains in the comfort zone when away – it's the camping version, putting it all in a pan and leaving to simmer. A little Parmesan is optional here – but unless the perfectionist in you got the upper hand when packing you're probably not going to have a grater. Finely sliced?

4 handfuls of spaghetti

Sauce
3 tablespoons extra virgin olive oil
½ teaspoon crushed garlic
6 canned anchovy fillets
1 x 14.5 oz can of chopped tomatoes
¼ teaspoon crushed dried red chili flakes
1 heaping tablespoon capers
4 tablespoons sliced green olives
sea salt

If you are reliant on a one ring stove, the sauce can be made in advance and reheated. Heat the olive oil in a medium saucepan, add the garlic and anchovies and cook for a minute, mashing the anchovies into a paste. Add all the remaining sauce ingredients and simmer for 10–15 minutes, until soft and thickened.

Boil the spaghetti in plenty of salted water until al dente, then drain it, return it to the pan and toss with the hot puttanesca sauce.

Equipment Stove, 2 saucepans

SYRIAN GRAIN SOUP

For 4–6 people

The first day we took our little sail boat on a jaunt down the river, we thought we would break ourselves in gently with "a day's camping." So we meandered and moored in a lovely spot, and I began to cook this simple Syrian grain soup, a recipe given to me by a friend, the food writer Nada Saleh.

As I was trying to get a grip on my new one ring stove by the river bank, I heard a large "crack" on the boat beside me, which was followed by an "oops," then a "damn it," and finally an "okay guys, I need help."

As it turned out, while I had been preparing lunch my husband had been tinkering with the outboard motor, which had fallen clear off the back of the boat. He had been left carrying the full weight of this iron beast when he realized that the boat was drifting away from the shore.

Normally calm under pressure would have typically been in control. But this was different, panic had taken over, "I can't hold it, I can't hold it, DO SOMETHING!"

I was trying: I had gotten back onto the boat, but now leapt onto the shore (as he had one foot in the boat and another on the shore and was doing a split that would impress any ballerina) and held him around the waist.

"Don't worry," I said, "I've got you."

Uttering some endearment he fell into the river and disappeared beneath the rippling water, heroically clutching the engine.

Mentally I had rehearsed the life-saving moves learned so many years earlier in a Red Cross swim program, but was dreading having to put them into practice on this day. Needless to say I was overcome with relief when he bobbed to the surface, still clutching the engine.

I returned to preparing this soup, a glamorized version of the simple rice soup they used to serve us every Friday at a Catholic convent where I

attended boarding school for a time in Belgium. Curiously you were also given a glass of beer with every lunch there, beginning at the age of five. That may not sound like much of a culinary pairing, but it's actually a delicious combination. It is those little secular touches that go to make this dish work in any event – the generous dousing with olive oil and lemon juice, some crusty bread and olives. Nada normally makes it with water, though I like to sneak in a little chicken stock or a bouillon cube to give it a boost.

extra virgin olive oil
1 onion, peeled, halved and finely sliced
1 level teaspoon Middle Eastern Spice Blend (see page 29)
$^1/_3$ mug of green lentils
$^1/_3$ mug of basmati rice
$^1/_3$ mug of bulghar wheat
sea salt
lemon juice

Heat a few tablespoons of oil in a medium or large saucepan and cook the onion over moderate heat until lightly browned. Stir in the spice blend, then add the lentils, rice and bulghar. Add 5 mugs of water and a bouillon cube if desired (see intro) and some salt. Bring to a boil, skim any foam from the surface, then partially cover with a lid and allow to simmer for 20 minutes, or until the grains are tender. Dish it up with some olive oil drizzled over the top and a squeeze of lemon juice.

Equipment Stove, saucepan

HOT DOG GOULASH

For 4 people

A variation on the theme of the British classic "bangers and mash," hot dogs are great camping material, as they don't require any grilling or frying. This is real soul food, the sort of dish any ravenous crew would welcome at the end of an active day outdoors.

4 or 5 strips of uncooked bacon, chopped
3 large onions, peeled, halved and sliced
8 medium new potatoes, scrubbed or peeled
12 hot dogs
a couple of bay leaves
sea salt and black pepper
1 mug of chicken stock

Heat a large saucepan or pot over medium heat, add the chopped bacon and cook in the rendered fat until golden. Add the onions and continue to cook, stirring frequently, until caramelized. Add the potatoes, hot dogs, bay leaves and some seasoning and gently mix. Pour in the chicken stock and gently simmer, covered, for 30–45 minutes, or until the potatoes are tender and sitting in a rich gravy – but keep an eye on it towards the end of the cooking to make sure it doesn't get too dry.

Equipment Stove or tripod, saucepan or pot

MY BIG FAT CHILI CON CARNE

For 6 people

It was my brother, a veteran camper, who told me how some friend of his had cooked up chili with rice in a big cast-iron pot on a camping trip for five families, effortlessly, and I thought "what a great idea." It makes the perfect supper for a cool evening. It's fantastic with guacamole (see page 86), or a simple avocado salad.

2 tablespoons vegetable oil
2 onions, peeled and finely chopped
1 teaspoon crushed garlic
2 teaspoons Middle Eastern Spice Blend (see page 29)
1½ pounds ground beef
2 x 14½-ounce cans of diced tomatoes
1 tablespoon tomato paste
1 teaspoon herbes de Provence (optional)
sea salt
1 x 15-ounce can of kidney beans, drained
savory rice (see page 151), and, if you like, guacamole (see page 86), sour cream and
  tortilla chips

Heat the oil in a large saucepan or pot over medium heat and cook the onions until softened (10–12 minutes) giving them a stir every now and then, and then add the garlic. Continue to cook until slightly golden. Stir in the spice blend and the ground beef, turn up the heat and continue to cook, breaking up the meat with a spoon, until browned.

Add the diced tomatoes, tomato paste, herbes de Provence if including, and some salt, then bring to a simmer and cook over low heat for about an hour, adding the beans halfway through.

Serve with an equally big pot of savory rice and any toppings you desire.

Equipment Stove or tripod, saucepan or pot

LAMB, BARLEY AND ROSEMARY STEW

For 6 people

Just a few adaptations to make this favorite camping-friendly. First, there is no real need to peel the potatoes, or the carrots, and if you are using baby carrots they won't require any cutting either. Nor is there any need to slice the meat – it simmers down to fork-tenderness and can be pulled apart once it's cooked. When at home, to avoid biting on bitter rosemary needles once the stew is cooked, I normally wrap the sprig in a small square of cheesecloth, something you are very unlikely to have on hand in a field kitchen. But if you have teabags on hand, simply cut off the top one, empty out the tea, pop the rosemary inside and fold the top down. Problem solved.

2 pounds lamb cubes for stew
3 onions, peeled, halved and thinly sliced
½ mug of pearl barley
sea salt and black pepper
1 sprig of fresh rosemary
2 chicken bouillon cubes
2 mugs of small carrots

6 small new potatoes, scrubbed or peeled as necessary, and halved or quartered lengthways
coarsely chopped fresh flat-leaf parsley to serve

Layer the lamb, onions and barley in a large saucepan or pot, seasoning the ingredients as you go, and tuck in the rosemary. Pour in 4 mugs of water, filling the mug within an inch of the top, crumble in the bouillon cubes, and press the ingredients down to submerge them. Bring to a boil and skim off any foam on the surface, then cover and cook over low heat for 1 hour. Stir in the carrots and potatoes and cook for another 30 minutes. Season to taste, and serve with chopped parsley scattered over the top. The stew can also be made in advance and reheated.

Equipment Stove or tripod, saucepan or pot

STEAMED MUSSELS

This makes for great communal eating, and a beach is just about the perfect place, where the mussels can either be cooked on a tripod or in a large pan over a portable gas stove.

Allow about 1 pound of **mussels** per person. Rinse and pick through them, pulling off the beards and discarding any that don't close when sharply tapped. Bring a glass of **white wine** to a boil with a few finely chopped **shallots** in a large saucepan or pot, add the mussels, cover, and steam them for 5 minutes or so until they open, stirring or shaking the pan halfway through.

Equipment Stove or tripod, saucepan or pot

TUMBET

For 6 people

This Spanish vegetable dish is very similar to ratatouille, but there is actually very little to saute here except for the eggplant, which tastes better when cooked in a hot pan before being added to the pot. This is lovely with most offerings from the grill (see page 111), or, for those who don't eat meat, with some grilled goat cheese.

extra virgin olive oil
1 large eggplant, trimmed and cut into chunks
2 onions, peeled and finely sliced
5 medium new potatoes, thickly sliced
2 red peppers, cored and seeds removed, cut into wide strips
2 zucchini, ends removed, thickly sliced
6 garlic cloves, peeled and chopped
2 beefsteak tomatoes, sliced
a couple of handfuls of fresh marjoram leaves or chopped
   fresh parsley, and extra to serve
½ mug of white wine
sea salt and black pepper

Cover the bottom of a large saucepan or pot with olive oil, place over medium–high heat and saute the eggplant chunks until lightly golden – you can add a drop more oil when turning them to get good color going on both sides. Add the rest of the ingredients with 1/3 of a mug of oil and give everything a stir. Once the liquid comes to a boil, cover and cook over low heat for 1–1¼ hours, or until the potatoes are tender, stirring halfway through. There will be lots of juices, so turn the heat up slightly and continue to cook, uncovered, until the juices concentrate by about a third, another 15 minutes or so. Serve with more herbs scattered on top.

Equipment Stove or tripod, saucepan or pot

ANDY WARHOL CHICKEN STEW

For 3–4 people

Taking a spaghetti sauce for your first night away is one route to calming frazzled nerves. It's just not very "camping", whereas this stew is at least a stab at something homemade. It is pretty much what you might imagine from the title, and very fine too in a faux-1960s-dinner-party way. A can of mushroom soup forms the basis of a sauce for chicken (using "tenders" ensures that there is no chopping to be done). A little fresh parsley at the end works wonders to whisk it back into the gourmet world. Tomorrow we will wake up feeling totally refreshed, the sun will be shining, and we will cook, properly.

a few tablespoons of vegetable or olive oil
a couple of handfuls of chopped, uncooked bacon
a couple of handfuls of button mushrooms
1 pound of small chicken fillets or "tenders"
$^1/_3$ mug of white wine
1 can of cream of mushroom soup
sea salt and black pepper
chopped fresh parsley or watercress

Heat the oil in a large saucepan or pot over medium heat and cook the bacon with the mushrooms until lightly golden. Stir in the chicken, then add the wine and simmer to reduce it by about half. Add the soup, a little salt and some pepper and simmer the mixture, covered, for 10 minutes, until the chicken is just tender and cooked through. Stir in a handful or two of chopped parsley or watercress.

To eat
Savory Rice (see page 151) or buttered potatoes.

Equipment Stove or tripod, saucepan or pot

CHICKEN TAGINE WITH PINE NUTS AND RAISINS

For 4–6 people

While a chicken typically serves about 4 people – the beauty of a tagine is that it is as much gravy and juices as it is meat, so this will stretch a chicken to feed 6. This recipe would also be good for guinea hen, either one nice large one or a couple of small ones.

1 free-range chicken (around 3 pounds), divided into pieces
2 beefsteak tomatoes, cored and sliced
2 onions, peeled and chopped
1 mug of red wine
2 teaspoons Moroccan Spice Blend (see page 29)
sea salt and black pepper
a handful of pine nuts
a handful of raisins

Combine all the ingredients except for the pine nuts and raisins in a large saucepan or pot. Bring to a boil, cover and cook gently for 1 hour, stirring in the pine nuts and raisins 15 minutes before the end.

To eat
Chopped cilantro, couscous or quinoa, or warm pita bread.

Equipment Stove or tripod, saucepan or pot

POT-ROAST PORK SHOULDER WITH ANCHOVIES AND FENNEL

For 6–8 people

A big-impact roast that serves a decent number of people, and very inexpensively. The meat is exquisitely tender by the end, hardly recognizable as pork at all, more like veal. At home I would sear the outside to brown it before cooking, but it is sufficiently lavish, with its anchovy and fennel sauce, without doing so.

Fennel is a plant that grows bountifully in the wild and is easily recognized by the most timid of foragers, with its luminous umbrella-shaped flowering heads and familiar feathery fronds. A few of these fronds, along with some of the young fresh seeds scattered over the pork at the end, will give it a little extra allure.

extra virgin olive oil
10 canned anchovy fillets
$^1/_3$ teaspoon dried crushed red chili flakes
sea salt and black pepper
1 x 3–4 pound pork shoulder
6 garlic cloves, peeled
1½ mugs of white wine
2 fennel bulbs, outer layer discarded, halved lenthwise and sliced

Drizzle a few tablespoons of oil over the bottom of a large saucepan or pot. Arrange the anchovy fillets in a single layer, sprinkle in the chili flakes, then season the pork all over and place it fat side down on top of the anchovies. Add the garlic cloves to the pan and pour in a mug of wine. Bring to a boil, then reduce the heat, cover and simmer over low heat for 2½ hours in total, until the meat is meltingly tender. Turn the meat and add the remaining ½ mug of wine after the first hour, and add the fennel about 30 minutes before the end of cooking. Skim the juices of fat off the top before serving.

To eat
Some warm bread and a large green salad are just as good here as a side of potatoes.

Equipment Stove or tripod, saucepan or pot

COWBOY COFFEE BEEF

For 4–6 people

When our son Louis was very small he bypassed the usual first-word stage and went straight to sentences. Every morning he would sit on our bed and say, "Corffee? No tank you corffee," which has always amazed us. Not because he spoke in sentences, but because neither of us could think of a single occasion that when offered a cup of coffee in bed we would have said "no." Especially when camping, it is the greatest of small luxuries.

Hang on to the rest of the coffee pot for this beef. It is a curiosity, though because by the end of cooking there isn't the slightest hint of the coffee, just a rich beef broth. This is more liquid than I would normally start off with, but I'm allowing for cooking over a slightly higher heat than normal – very low flames have a habit of blowing out. The gravy won't go to waste with some buttery potatoes, while pasta and rice make equally fine partners.

about 2 pounds stew meat, cut into pieces, ideally the size of a plum
1½ mugs of coffee
1½ mugs of red wine
1 head of garlic, top cut off, papery skin removed
a couple of bay leaves
sea salt
a large pinch of dried red chili flakes or black pepper
4 large carrots, peeled and thickly sliced
a couple of handfuls of shallots, peeled

Place the beef in a large saucepan or pot with the coffee, wine, garlic, bay leaves, salt and chili or black pepper. Bring to a boil, skim off any foam and simmer covered for 2 hours, adding the carrots and shallots halfway through. Everything should be meltingly tender by the end. The inside of the cooked garlic can be squeezed out and mashed into the juices.

To eat
Buttered pasta, rice or potatoes.

Equipment Stove or tripod, saucepan or pot

THE GRILL

When we're at home we play with our grill, whereas when we're camping we live with it. There is something exciting about being reliant on an open fire to cook with, rather than knowing you can always finish off whatever you're grilling indoors if everything goes wrong. The hardcore camping approach where you start from scratch, building a little fire with wood, protecting it from the wind with rocks, is hugely satisfying. It's very easy, and opens the door not just for grilling but for one-pot cooking also. This is assuming that you are camping somewhere that it is allowed, and sadly as land becomes more restricted and regulated the opportunities are fewer. So a little traveling grill is a good safety net when the great outdoors doesn't allow for such fun.

My portable grill is the first item I take out to pack, and it sits there like an expectant dog waiting for a walk, long before any other essentials, like a tent, have even been thought about. This and a camping stove are the foundation of the traveler's kitchen. I've explored the choices in a little more detail in the chapter "Essential Kit" (see pages 13–16), but ultimately I encourage you to go for a mini-kettle type or covered grill. This provides an all-weather solution – if it's pouring or very windy, you will still be able to create a gorgeous shoulder of lamb or sticky roast chicken. I know this from experience: I have been soaked through, freezing cold and close to tears and dinner has still been fantastic, surreally at odds with the conditions. And suddenly it all seems worth it again.

The second justification for a covered grill is having the ability to roast larger cuts by creating a kind of oven, and that broadens your options. That said, there is no reason why you can't cook any of the small cuts here on an open grill (provided the weather is fine), and fend off any flare-ups with the occasional splash of water.

If I was allowed to take everything on my wish list (this one's always down to negotiation), I would pack a chimney starter too (see page 15). These don't come small, so you might have to do some fairly serious bargaining, but they are foolproof for the fire-shy. Just stuff a couple pieces of newspaper into the base, light it with your coals in the chimney above and 30 to 40 minutes later they will be blazing away.

I'd like to sneak in that one final tip, something I always forget as it goes against nature – start a little bit earlier than you think you need to. For some reason grills always take longer than anticipated, I find most charcoal brands suggest that coals will be ready in half the time it actually takes to get really hot before you start cooking. If the directions claim 20 minutes, then I would give it 45. Wait until the coals are well-coated in a fine layer of grey ash, moving them around if necessary. If you put the food on and cover the grill when they are only half-coated in ash, there is a good chance they will stay that way. No amount of guitar playing around the campfire is going to soothe the wounded pride of the cook.

OYSTERS WITH GARLIC BUTTER

While looking at a box of **oysters** sitting beside the tent one day (often one of the great treats when you are camping close to cooler coastal areas), I thought, "There has to be an easy way in there." And then, "Given that mussels steam open on the grill, as do clams, why shouldn't oysters?" And they do, on a very hot covered grill, oysters behave like any other tenacious bivalve.

Timing is everything, however. Three minutes on a covered grill over high heat and just a few will have started to peek open; give it 4 minutes and they should all be open, retaining that slippery delicacy which draws us to them when we serve them raw. However a minute or so beyond this and they will turn chewy. So place them curve side down and cook them just long enough to be able to slip a knife into the crack and lever the shell open.

While they are grilling (or you are opening them up), melt some **garlic butter** (see page 150) in a small pan. Lift off the flat side of the shell, and with it the oyster, pour any juices into the curved half and spoon the melted butter over the top.

Equipment Grill, saucepan

GOAT CHEESE WRAPPED IN PROSCIUTTO

For about 6 people as an appetizer, or 3 as a light lunch or dinner

You can serve this with some toasted sourdough bread, a little green salad, and sun-dried tomatoes.

5–6 slices of Prosciutto or other air-dried ham
1 x approx. 6-inch medium-mature goat cheese log

First wrap a slice of Prosciutto around each end of the cheese, and then

wind the remainder around the middle. The idea is to contain the melted cheese so it doesn't drip onto the grill – but don't worry if you find a little works its way out as you're cooking.

Cook on the grid of a hot grill until golden all over. The cheese should be melted around the edges, and warm and mousse-like within.

To eat
Crackers or warmed pita wedges.

Equipment Grill

MUSTARD AND HONEY COCKTAIL SAUSAGES

For 4 people

Strange, given how good cocktail sausages are, how curiously hard they can be to find. But the solution is simple – buy some thin Italian sausages, give each one about 4 twists in the center, as if making a balloon animal at a children's party, and cut into cocktail sausages.

Thread 1 pound of **cocktail sausages** onto flat metal skewers, piercing them through the middle (as opposed to lengthwise), leaving a little space between them so they can cook evenly. Grill them for 5–10 minutes, until half-cooked, turning them as necessary and moving them to the outside of the grid if they appear to be browning too quickly. Brush with 2 tablespoons of **Camping Glaze** (see page 28) and grill for another 5–10 minutes until golden and sticky. The glaze will brown very quickly, so keep an eye on them.

Equipment Grill, metal skewers

GLAMPING SAUSAGES

This one's good for a crowd, especially all those chic bohemian friends who are expecting more from you than a sausage on a stick.

You want a really meaty sausage here. Grill as many **sausages** as you need on a grill or over a fire. I find these normally take about 20 minutes, and there's no need to oil or prick them. At the same time open lots of **oysters** (or grill these too, see page 114), and serve the two together with a big pot of **Crushed Potatoes** (see page 148) and a **green salad** (see page 136).

Equipment Grill

GRILLED PORK CHOPS WITH AIOLI

For 4 people

Pork chops cook up beautifully on a grill: the ideal are the really nice fat, juicy ones, which will be divine with this pungent aioli sauce.

4 juicy pork chops
extra virgin olive oil
4 sprigs of fresh rosemary
6 sprigs of fresh thyme
6 tablespoons mayonnaise
4 tablespoons Camping Marinade (see page 27)
sea salt and black pepper

About an hour before grilling, marinate the chops in a bowl or container with a few tablespoons of olive oil and the needles and leaves from the rosemary and thyme. To make the aioli, put the mayonnaise and Camping Marinade into a bowl and blend with a spoon.

Season the chops and cook for a few minutes each side over a very hot grill, until golden and firm when pressed. Serve with the aioli.

Equipment Grill

MIDDLE EASTERN LAMB CHOPS

For 4 people

Delicious with A Kind of Baba Ghanoush (see page 142) and Smoky Zucchini Salad (see page 137).

8 juicy lamb cutlets or chops
8 tablespoons Camping Marinade (see page 27)
2 teaspoons Middle Eastern Spice Blend (see page 29)

About an hour before grilling, put the chops into a bowl or container with the Camping Marinade and spice blend and leave to marinate.

Cook the chops for a few minutes on each side over a very hot grill until golden, but with a slight give to leave them, for medium-rare.

Extra thyme
If you have a few stalks of fresh thyme with you, strip half the leaves off and spinkle these and the stalks over the chops while grilling.

Equipment Grill

JERK CHICKEN

For 4 people

The smell of jerk chicken sizzling on a grill is one of my favorite summer scents. The spicy, sticky finish is worth making the trip altogether. Chicken breast fillets or chicken "tenders" are the ideal here, because they cook fast and evenly, whereas legs and drumsticks take longer and need to be watched carefully to prevent them from drying out before they are fully cooked in the middle.

4 tablespoons Camping Marinade (see page 27)
2 teaspoons Jerk Seasoning (see page 29)
chicken fillets to serve 4

A couple of hours before grilling, combine the marinade with the Jerk Seasoning in a bowl or airtight container, then add the chicken and coat it. Cover and set aside if not cooking right away. Grill over hot coals for a few minutes each side – the chicken should feel firm when pressed, and don't worry if it isn't deeply golden all over, pale will do. The important thing is to catch it while it's still moist and succulent.

Equipment Grill

GRILLED SARDINES

For 4 people

Taking in the scent of sardines grilling outdoors is one of the best ways of transporting yourself to some warm Mediterranean shore. It's a delicious feast with a juicy tomato salad and some buttered whole grain bread, or perhaps a couscous salad. Sardines are very delicate little fish – one reason why some fishmongers won't gut them for you (though it's worth asking) – and they also tend to come off the grill looking a little ragged, which I don't mind, but one of those fish clamps will preserve their silvery form and will save you from having to turn them individually, in which case you may need to allow an extra minute or so. The grill plate of a Cobb grill also offers a non-stick surface and leaves the sardines intact.

8 good-sized sardines, cleaned and scaled
6 tablespoons Camping Marinade
    (see page 27)
½–1 teaspoon Moroccan Spice Blend
    (see page 29)

You can ask your fishmonger to scale the sardines for you, though they'll probably still need a good wash to completely remove the scales. Pat them dry.

Pour the Camping Marinade over the sardines in a large bowl, sprinkle with the Moroccan Spice Blend and turn the fish to coat using your hands. Cook on a grill for a few minutes each side, until golden and the fish easily comes away from the backbone.

Equipment Grill, fish clamp (optional)

FISH BAKED IN NEWSPAPER

In our camp we're rather fond of this frontier method, which indulges us the fantasy that we're camping wild somewhere in the mountains with nothing more than a fishing rod and a good newspaper for company.

This way of cooking small, whole fish has the same austerity as steaming them between long wild grasses (see page 126): it keeps the flesh beautifully moist and traps every ounce of the fish's flavor within the paper shell. Like so many radically simple dishes, however, it is not necessarily the easiest to get right. It is often suggested that the packets are baked in the embers of a fire, but the dividing line between embers and ashes is a fine one. It's not the kind of dish you can test halfway through, as once the packet is open you have to proceed with eating it. I would serve the fish with Campfire Tagine Tomato Sauce (see page 144), fresh lemon slices, pita bread and also, in a perfect world, some hot, buttered asparagus.

Any small fish are candidates, but I have a particular soft spot for **red snapper and sea bass**, each offering a buttery sweetness with a firm succulence. A couple of fish weighing in at a pound or so each will be sufficient for 4 people, although that said, you'll probably polish them off even if there are only 2 of you. You probably want about 6 ounces per person of filleted fish, so allow double that for a whole, unfilleted fish.

Season each fish liberally with **sea salt**, including the cavity, and wrap in about 5 sheets of **newspaper**, wetting each sheet first. This provides a more secure packet than if you simply wet a stack of paper. Cook the packets for about 15 minutes on each side on a covered grill – there is not a chance of the paper actually bursting into flames, even though you might think there is, but you may need to splash a bit of water at the packets now and then if the edges of the paper start to smoke. By the end the newspaper will be blackened, but once cut open the skin of the fish should come away with the paper, revealing beautifully cooked milky white flesh.

Equipment Grill

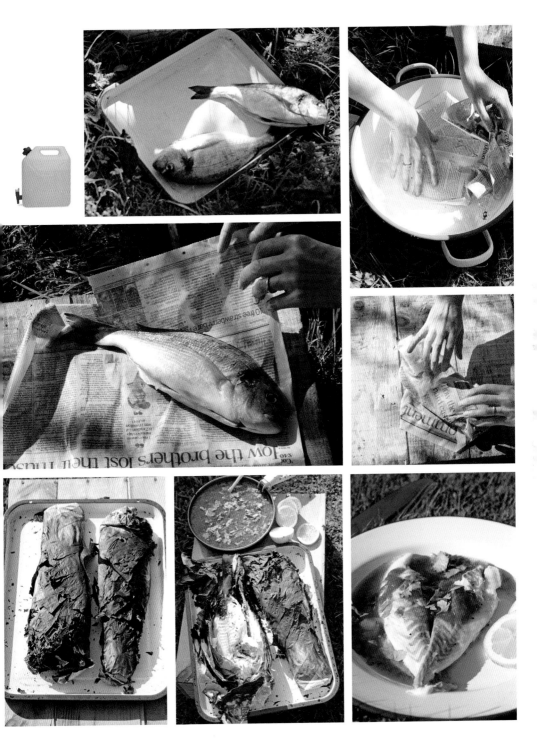

WHOLE FISH STEAMED BETWEEN WILD GRASSES

A lovely way of cooking any whole fish, where long wild grasses scent the flesh as it grills, keeping it moist at the same time. **Salmon, trout, or sea bass** are all good candidates. A salmon will take around 30 minutes per side, while something smaller should take around 20 minutes per side. As with Fish Baked in Newspaper (see page 124), allow about 1–1½ pounds of whole, unfilleted fish for 2 people.

When at the market, ask for the fish to be gutted and scaled. Now season it well with **sea salt and pepper both** inside and out. You can also score the flesh diagonally and stuff the slits with some chopped herbs – **chives, parsley, tarragon** will all be good – and some finely grated **lemon zest** and seasoning. Keep any adornment as simple as the fish: an **herb mayonnaise**, or **butter** melted with **herbs** and a little **lemon**.

Moisten an armful of **long wild grasses** and spread half of them over the grid of your grill, covering it well. Lay the fish on top and spread the remaining grasses on top so that the fish is completely nested within. The grass will hiss as the fish is steamed. Keep the grass moist by splashing it with water when necessary.

Equipment Grill

ROAST LAMB WITH SWEET AND SOUR TOMATO SAUCE 🍖

For 4 people

Half a lamb shoulder is a good compact roast that should fit on a traveling kettle grill. That said, I've also successfully prepared a whole shoulder in a Cobb grill, by first browning it for about 15 minutes skin side down, then cooking it the other way up for 1½ hours in total. Pop some bread onto the grill just before eating – the sauce is deliciously soupy, so there's lots of dunking to be done. I'd grill some big portobello mushrooms at the same time, as a side vegetable.

sea salt and black pepper
½ a lamb shoulder
fresh rosemary sprigs
3 tomatoes, preferably "on-the-vine"
2 tong-tips (i.e. 2 tablespoons) of tomato chutney
extra virgin olive oil

Season the lamb shoulder all over and place it on the grid of a kettle grill (e.g. a Weber using the "indirect" method). Scatter some rosemary needles and sprigs over the roast, rubbing them into the surface of the meat. Close the lid and grill for about 1 hour, turning the the lamb halfway through – it should be pink in the center. Leave to rest for 15 minutes, then carve.

About 30 minutes before the lamb is ready, place the tomatoes beside the lamb. Remove them at the same time as the lamb, leave to cool a little and then remove the skins. Pull the tomato flesh away from the cores and put into a bowl. Add the chutney, a little salt, and a few dashes of olive oil. Serve with the lamb.

Equipment Grill

BUTTERFLIED LEG OF LAMB

For 6 people, or 8 as a glorified sandwich

A butterflied leg of lamb is a great cut, like a big juicy fillet – it cooks in no time at all, and it's one of the barbecue treats of the summer. A whole butterflied leg spreads itself out and requires a large kettle grill to cook it on, which is not to stop you from cutting it in half and cooking it in two stages on a traveling kettle grill. It's equally delicious after having cooled down as it is eaten hot off the grill. It makes for great DIY entertaining for a number of people: all you have to do is lay out a selection of breads, a green salad, and perhaps the aioli on page 120.

1 leg of lamb, approx. 5-6 pounds, butterflied
5 tablespoons Camping Marinade (see page 27)
1 heaping tablespoon fresh thyme leaves
sea salt and black pepper

Open out the butterflied leg of lamb, cut it in half, place the two halves in a bowl or dish and using your hands, coat it on both sides with the Camping Marinade and the thyme.

Season the lamb and cook one half at a time in a covered kettle grill (e.g. a Weber using the "indirect" method), allowing about 20 minutes per side, and placing it skin down first. Timing is always an inexact art, so use this as a rough guide – if you stick a knife into the thickest part it should still appear pink. Set this half aside while you cook the second half – first adding another few briquettes to each side of the grill, and leaving about 15 minutes for them to heat up. Slice the lamb across the grain, spooning any juices over the meat.

Equipment Grill

STICKY ROAST CHICKEN

For 4–5 people

A whole roast chicken when home seems almost mundane – but transported outdoors it is as comforting as a down duvet and a pair of sheepskin slippers. It is also, somehow, a reminder that we haven't left all civilization at home. This plays on the Cobb grill's great strength of cooking a whole bird along with potatoes – although the maximum size of chicken to go for is 3½ pounds. As for the potatoes, which are a cross between roasted and baked, you want smallish waxy ones rather than large baking potatoes, so they will cook through easily. Serving with The Very Chunky Mushroom Sauce on page 145 would be my recommendation, and it doubles up as a veggie too.

Anything else? Well, the Sweet Little Peas on page 139 are next on the wish list.

If, however, you don't have a Cobb, a traveling Weber using the "indirect" method (see page 14) is another solution. Halve the chicken as though butterflying it, cutting first through the base and then the breastbone, which you can remove if you wish. Drizzle with a little oil, season, then coat the chicken with the glaze and grill it, covered, for 45 minutes, skin-side-down for half the time and then turning over half way through. This is also a lovely way of cooking a guinea hen. These tend to be smaller – a good-sized one of 2-3 pounds will serve 4 people max.

vegetable or olive oil
1 x 3-4 pound free-range chicken (untrussed)
sea salt and black pepper
2 tablespoons Camping Glaze (see page 28)
8 medium new potatoes, scrubbed

Drizzle a little oil over your chicken and season it. Grill it on either a roasting rack or on the grill plate of a Cobb grill for 1½ hours – giving it 10 minutes on each breast initially to brown it before turning it the right way up. Drizzle with the Camping Glaze halfway through.

At the same time, rub the potatoes with oil, season with salt and cook them around the bird, turning them halfway through when you glaze the chicken. You can leave these on the grill while you rest the chicken for 15–20 minutes, rearranging them so that they cook evenly.

Equipment Grill

SIDE ORDERS

A passion for vegetables doesn't diminish just while camping, it simply gets a little trickier to deliver all those lovely sides that we take for granted when we're at home. Fear not though, because nothing that follows is even vaguely challenging.

Starting with the no-cook route, a green salad and a stack of warm bread are the quickest way of rounding out any menu, and they are often the most welcome. With this approach the Camping Marinade (see page 27) and Camping Glaze (see page 28) score large points – combine the two and you have a sophisticated little salad dressing with the hints of garlic, mustard and honey that are so central to a good vinaigrette. Take along a couple of spare lockable plastic containers and you can bring along plenty without the risk of it leaking while you are on the move.

Next, with the kind of relaxed fare we're after, we need to involve the grill. It offers up all sorts of inspired fare, starting with Provençal vegetables, the trio of eggplant, zucchini

and tomatoes, all of which can be thrown onto the grill whole, and are readily served up once cooked into delightful dishes with the help of the Camping Marinade and a few spices.

Over on the one-pot front, Smothered Green Beans (see page 141) are a huge favorite, and in fact I could happily eat these with every meal – a little stew where tomatoes, onions and garlic fuse into a rich sauce that coats whatever green or yellow beans you have to hand.

On to carbs. We need these when we're camping. Being pleasantly satiated is no longer enough, we need to feel "full." The very simplest carb is couscous: simply add boiling water, a few rounds of olive oil and some salt and ten minutes later it's ready for devouring while hot with soupy stews, or at a later date, served cold in a salad. This way of cooking couscous, in which it cooks by the "absorption method", doesn't sound very alluring but in practice it leaves you with perfectly fluffy grains and a clean pan, while Crushed Potatoes are the answer to "mashed", and suitably rustic. Or why not make some garlic bread, a friend to pretty much any meal, but especially with My Big Fat Chili con Carne (see page 98) and No-chop Spaghetti Puttanesca (see page 93).

There are also a couple of ideas for sauces, in Campfire Tagine Tomato Sauce (see page 144) big tomatoes are filled with spices, garlic and olive oil and cooked on the grill until soft. Scoop out the insides and you have a ready-made sauce. Or grill mushrooms filled with crème fraîche, then coarsely chop them, and the juices combine with the cream to create a lovely, chunky sauce that's especially good with chicken and grilled fish. As always, don't wait to go camping to enjoy the ease of these – a barbeque in the backyard is just as good of an opportunity.

SOMETHING GREEN

THE SIMPLE SOLUTION

The easiest route to rounding out any grilled or one-pot meal is to serve a big green salad and lots of bread, neither of which will hog the grill or that one precious ring.

BREAD

If your bread is fresh there's nothing more to do, but the greatest convenience when camping is to bring various flatbreads that can be warmed on the grill for a minute or two after you have taken whatever you are cooking off it, or in a pan on a gas ring for an equally short amount of time. They keep for days, and it goes without saying that they can't get squashed.

A GREEN SALAD

Lovely as big leafy **lettuces** are, they take a lot of washing, and tightly closed hearts or heads are a better option. **Little Baby Lettuces**, **Romaine lettuce hearts** and **endive** are personal favorites. This is also the time to turn to bags of pre-washed leaves – I tend to favor one variety over the mixes, so **watercress**, **arugula** and **mache** are all good. You can mix these with leaves from other hearts or with a few **sprouts**.

A TOMATO SALAD

Tomato salads don't have to try very hard to be gorgeous, especially during the summer months. A serrated knife will make light work of any selection of **tomatoes** you have acquired. Season them with **salt**, drizzle with **extra virgin olive oil**, and scatter a little chopped **fresh parsley** or slices of **scallion** over the top, should you have either hanging around.

SMOKY ZUCCHINI SALAD

For 4 people

At home I painstakingly slice and then grill my zucchini, whereas here, to make life easier, they are grilled first and then cut up and dressed. You can make this dish even more substancial with some fresh goat cheese and black olives.

Drizzle some **extra virgin olive oil** over 6 small **zucchini** and season with **salt and pepper**. Grill for 20–40 minutes, until slightly golden and soft. Leave to cool for a bit, then cut off the ends, throw them into a bowl and coarsely chop. Add a few tablespoons of olive oil, a squeeze of **lemon juice**, some salt and pepper, and a handful of **pine nuts** and **freshly torn basil or mint leaves**. Eat slightly warm or at room temperature.

Equipment Grill

HONEY-MUSTARD SALAD DRESSING

Enough for a couple of salads for 3–4 people

Place 2 teaspoons of **Camping Glaze** (see page 28) in a small airtight container or jar with 6 tablespoons of **Camping Marinade** (see page 27), put the lid on and give it a good shake.

CUCUMBER AND FETA COUSCOUS

For 4 people

If you weren't into couscous before you started camping, you are about to start loving it. With no cooking involved, it is perfect for the occasion, makes great salads and is lovely with soupy tagines and stews.

1 mug of couscous
extra virgin olive oil
sea salt
½ a cucumber, quartered and thinly sliced
a few small fresh mint leaves, torn
6 tablespoons Camping Marinade (see page 27)
a couple of handfuls of pitted green olives
1 x 7-ounce block of feta cheese, coarsely crumbled

Combine the couscous, a tablespoon or two of olive oil and a pinch of salt in a large bowl, then pour in 1½ mugs of boiling water and set aside. It will be ready in 10 minutes, but for the purposes of this salad, leave it to cool and then fluff it up. Toss in all the remaining salad ingredients, adding the feta last. Drizzle with a little more oil before serving.

SWEET LITTLE PEAS

For 4 people

You could use frozen baby peas here by allowing them to sit out and defrost a bit first, however when camping, I find the canned versions too easy to pass up.

Empty a 15-ounce can of sweet peas in a medium-sized pan and add a little **butter**, a **sliced lettuce heart**, a sprig of **mint** if you have one. Cover and cook over low heat for 10 minutes.

Equipment Stove, saucepan

GRILLED CORN WITH SAGE AND LEMON

For 4 people

Drizzle some **extra virgin olive oil** over 4 **corn cobs**, shucked, and season them with **salt and pepper**. Grill for about 20 minutes, until nicely golden all over, then transfer them to a plate while you make the butter.

Place a large pan on to the grill and melt about ¾ of a stick of **unsalted butter**. Once the foam begins to settle, sprinkle in a handful of **sage leaves** and the grated **zest of a lemon** (though this is optional) over the surface and cook until the leaves darken and become crisp. Remove from the heat and stir in 5 tablespoons of extra virgin olive oil. Serve this spooned over the corn, with a squeeze of **lemon juice**, and a touch of sea salt. The sage leaves will be good to eat, while the lemon zest is there purely to scent.

Equipment Grill, large pan

FONDUE LEEKS

For 4 people as a side, or 2 people as a main

Like all good fondues you need to stand watch over these and be prepared to begin eating them the minute they come off the grill. Add to the menu some honey-roasted ham, and you have a feast of a supper.

Trim 8 good-sized **leeks** (or 4 if very large) and wipe down with a moist towel to remove any sand or grit. Drizzle with **extra virgin olive oil** and season with **salt and pepper**. Don't worry about removing the tough outer layers – these serve as a cooking shell and will be discarded. Cook on a covered grill for 20–30 minutes, turning them halfway through, until they are blackened on the outside and a knife inserted into them goes through with ease.

Slit the leeks open and arrange cut side up on one or two pieces of foil, cupping the edges. Drizzle with a little oil, season and cover with slices of **Gruyère**, **Beaufort** or **Emmental**. Drizzle with a little more oil, sprinkle with some fresh thyme leaves, slip the foil back on to the grill and cook covered for another 10 minutes, until the cheese has melted. Eat just the insides of the leeks with the melted cheese, discarding the charred exterior.

Equipment Grill, foil

SMOTHERED GREEN BEANS

For 4 people

The summer brings with it green beans of every variety – in the summer months, we can choose from yellow or green, skinny or fat. They travel well, don't require any cooling and call for minimum preparation. It's a pleasurable, idle 10 minutes spent sitting in the late afternoon sun snapping off the ends with your fingers.

1 large handful of green or yellow beans per person, ends trimmed, halved if long
2 tomatoes, sliced
2 garlic cloves, peeled and sliced
sea salt and black pepper
1 onion, peeled, halved and sliced
3 tablespoons extra virgin olive oil, plus extra for drizzling
a handful of chopped fresh parsley, chervil or chives (optional)

Throw everything except for the herbs into a medium saucepan, pop the lid on and cook over gentle heat for 30–40 minutes, checking on them occasionally, until the beans are tender and sitting in a light tomato sauce. Serve with a drizzle of oil and a sprinkle of herbs if you have any on hand.

Equipment Stove, saucepan

A KIND OF BABA GHANOUSH

For 4 people

Eggplant and tomatoes are two of the most successful vegetables to cook on a grill – they don't even require oil or seasoning – simply throw them on whole. The eggplant will take about 45 minutes to cook, so you will probably need to put these on before any meat that is part of the feast. This is delicious served with grilled, spicy sausages, and warm bread.

4 eggplants
3 tomatoes, preferably "on-the-vine"
3 tablespoons Camping Marinade (see page 27)
1 teaspoon Middle Eastern Spice Blend (optional) (see page 29)
sea salt
extra virgin olive oil
a handful of coarsely chopped fresh flat-leaf parsley

Prick the eggplants all over to prevent them from bursting, and grill for about 45 minutes until the skin is blackened and blistered, turning them now and again. Grill the tomatoes for about 20 minutes, turning them once. Leave both to cool a little, then skin the eggplants and coarsely chop the flesh in a bowl using a knife and fork. If there is any excess liquid pour it out, pressing it out using a fork. Skin the tomatoes and add the flesh to the bowl, crushing it with your fingers. Mix in the Camping Marinade, the spice blend and some salt, then splash with some oil and scatter the parsley over the top.

Equipment Grill

A COUPLE OF SAUCES

CAMPFIRE TAGINE TOMATO SAUCE

For 4 people

A deliciously smoky sauce for ladling over any grilled meat or fish, which is baked within the tomato shell. It can also be made in advance and gently reheated, adding the cilantro at the last minute.

3 good-sized beefsteak tomatoes
sea salt
1 teaspoon Moroccan Spice Blend (see page 29)
1 garlic clove, peeled and crushed to a paste
extra virgin olive oil
a handful of coarsely chopped fresh cilantro (optional)

Slice the top off each tomato and scoop out the core in the center, about 2 tablespoons of the flesh in total. Season the cut surface with salt, sprinkle the spice and garlic into the cavities, and refill with olive oil, almost to the top. Replace the "lid," place the tomatoes in a shallow pan such as a Trangia frying pan, and cook in a covered grill for 30–45 minutes until softened – you may find there is a pool of juices and some oil in the pan. You can also cook these over an open grid.

Scoop the softened flesh away from the shells, discarding the skin, and add the cilantro if you have some.

Equipment Grill, pan

A VERY CHUNKY MUSHROOM SAUCE

For 4 people

This is one of those sauces hearty enough to stand in as a vegetable, great for roast chicken in lieu of gravy or with grilled steaks and other meats. It neatly occupies the twenty minutes during which the meat is resting, and is especially appealing for late summer camping.

Drizzle some **extra virgin olive oil** over 4 **portobello mushrooms**, stalks discarded, and season them with **salt and black pepper**. Grill them on a covered grill cupped-side down for 10 minutes, then turn them, fill the cavities with **crème fraîche** and grill for another 10 minutes. Coarsely chop them in a bowl and add a handful of coarsely chopped **fresh flat-leaf parsley**.

Equipment Grill

A CARB ON THE SIDE

GARLIC ROSEMARY POTATOES

For 4 people

The two types of potato that will most challenge campers (and you WILL crave potatoes) are roasted and baked. These delicious taters, which are cooked skin on, cut a fine line between the two. The rosemary and garlic make for especially tasty spuds – there is, however, a pan to wash afterwards. Sorry about that.

a handful of small new potatoes per person, scrubbed
extra virgin olive oil
sea salt and black pepper
4 garlic cloves, peeled and halved
a few sprigs of fresh rosemary

Toss the potatoes in a large saucepan with enough olive oil to coat and some seasoning, then add the garlic and rosemary. Add about 6 tablespoons of water, cover and cook over low heat for 30 minutes or until tender. Keep an eye on them to make sure they haven't cooked themselves dry, and add a tad more water if they seem to need it – the idea basically is to steam them. Continue to cook uncovered until any residual water evaporates and the potatoes are golden brown.

Equipment Stove or tripod, saucepan or pot

BABY BAKED POTATOES

For 4 people

Another take on roasted-baked potatoes, this time cooked in foil on a grill – they absorb the wine and scent of the bay leaves and are lovely and oily on the outside.

But if you are simply after the most basic way of baking a potato, don't worry about the bay leaves, and water will stand in for wine.

a handful of baby potatoes per person
4 tablespoons extra virgin olive oil
4 tablespoons white wine
sea salt and black pepper
4 bay leaves

Divide the potatoes between two pieces of foil so they sit in a single layer. Drizzle with the oil and wine, season and tuck in the bay leaves. Wrap up into a packet, then place on a second piece of foil, seam-side down, and wrap up again. Cook in a covered grill for 1¼–1½ hours, turning the packets halfway through.

Epuipment Grill, foil

CRUSHED POTATOES

For 4 people

These potatoes are a good choice for when you want something in between boiled potatoes and a potato salad. They're delicious eaten hot or warm, and I also enjoy them cold.

new potatoes for 4 people, peeled or scrubbed as necessary
about 8 tablespoons extra virgin olive oil
a handful of chopped fresh parsley
sea salt

Cook the potatoes in boiling salted water until tender. Drain them in a colander and leave for a few minutes for the surface moisture to evaporate. Return the potatoes to the pan and, using a fork or the back of a spoon, gently crush them into pieces. Pour in the olive oil, sprinkle in the parsley and season with salt.

Equipment Stove, saucepan

GARLIC BREAD

For 1 small baguette

Garlic butter is a good one to make before you leave home and take with you in an airtight container. As well as being used for garlic bread, melted it makes a great sauce for all sorts of shellfish – grilled oysters and shrimp, clams, mussels – or simply grilled fish or chicken.

Blend about half a stick of **softened unsalted butter** with 2–3 crushed **garlic cloves** and some **salt and black pepper** – in an ideal world I would also add some chopped soft fresh herbs such as **parsley** or **chives**.

Either thickly slice the **baguette**, leaving the pieces attached at the base, and generously spread the butter on either side of each slice, or slit it in half horizontally and spread the butter from top to bottom. Depending on the size of your grill, you may need to halve it first. Wrap it up in foil. Heat it on the grid of a grill or in a pan on a stove for about 5 minutes each side.

Equipment Grill, or stove and pan, foil

SAVORY RICE

For 4 people

A great method for cooking rice when camping. By a simple absorption process, you should be left with a pretty clean pan at the end. You can spice this up with chicken or vegetable stock, and serve the rice plain or add whatever suits your taste – some slivers of roasted vegetables, crispy bacon, toasted nuts, or chopped herbs and olive oil. It can be eaten hot, or used for salads once it's cool.

1¾ mugs of water or chicken or vegetable stock
1 tin mug of basmati rice
1 teaspoon sea salt

Add the stock, rice and salt to a medium saucepan. Bring the liquid to the boil and simmer for 8–10 minutes, then cover the pan, remove from the heat and leave to stand for 20 minutes. Fluff the rice up with a fork to serve.

Equipment Stove, saucepan

SWEET CHIC

It is easy to see why marshmallows (and bananas) are the camping hit that they are, as they capture the moment after supper so perfectly, when you want something sweet to finish with, but ideally without having to lift a finger – not least because it is getting dark and you can't see what you're doing. If you're not careful you risk waking up to colonies of ants marching purposefully through your tent. So this chapter is really an extension of that way of thinking, which shamelessly exploits any sweet (and fruit) that is up for being grilled, not just marshmallows but those bons-bons, nougat and even jelly babies.

One of the best ways of showing your age is to recall how much per piece the candies were at your local general store. The walls lined with large jars, served by a lady behind a counter who placed them in a brown paper bag. But frankly you don't have to be that old. It's simply that these days it seems you have to go to department or specialty stores for them, or online to some lavish website. Otherwise you are most likely to find such delights in some hidden-away corner shop in the middle of nowhere, forgotten by time.

Seeking out these small treasures are worth it when camping though. Tiny, portable and surprisingly good when heated over the campfire. Tiny, portable and surprisingly good when heated over the campfire, try warming sugar-dusted sweets with toffee inside to make a great brûlée topping. And good ole grilled bananas are always a winner, blackened over the grill, then slit and filled with the chocolate of your choice; while pretty much any fruit, and in particular stone fruits and figs, will be divine dipped into water and then into sugar and grilled until they caramelize.

If you insist that it has to be a real, full-on dessert, I would suggest wrapping a hunk of cake (such as the chocolate or ginger cakes on pages 59 and 65) in foil and warming it for about 5 minutes on either side on the grill or in a pan – *et voilà*, a sponge cake that you can drizzle with syrup or eat with a splash of cream.

SOUR PATCH KID SKEWERS

Something of a Joan of Arc moment here, but thread 4 **sour patch kids**, of different flavors, through the MIDDLE on to a metal or soaked wooden skewer. Gently heat them close to the embers of a fire – a grill in its dying hour will do fine. You need to catch them just at the right moment, while they still have the composure of their shape, but are liquid gel within, the consistency of one of those beautiful glacé fruits, that drips with a viscous syrup once you're past its candied shell.

Equipment Grill, skewers

STRAWBERRY SAUCERS

Never could I have dreamt up a dessert involving flying saucers – it took a child's mind to accommodate the fact that he had to get something healthy in there, if he wanted sweets at all.

Invest in a large jar of chalky, retro pastel-colored **flying saucers** – orange and lemon yellow, dusky pink and green. Tap each one to shake the tiny, balled candies inside to the bottom of the shell, then cut off the top and top with a sliver of **strawberry**.

STICKY FIGS

Figs are especially good grilled in this manner. Anything cooked on a grill will acquire a slightly smoky scent, but it's not unpleasing, especially if you pair it with a young goat cheese.

Cut in half and then dip a couple of **figs** per person first into water (or lemon juice) and then into **sugar**. Grill either side, cut-side down first, until sticky and golden, and serve with a dollop of **young goat cheese**.

You could also serve the figs with warm ginger cake instead of the cheese – lovely if there's any left over from the children's picnic (see page 65) earlier in the day. To warm the cake, wrap it in foil and place it on the grid of a grill for about 5 minutes on either side.

Equipment Grill

BON-BON BRÛLÉES

For this you want the old-fashioned **sugared bons-bons** with toffee inside.
Allow a couple per person, popped onto the end of skewers. Grill over
a grill or an open fire until the sugar on the outside has caramelized,
meaning that the toffee within will have melted into a delightful goo. Slip
this on top of a small cup of **vanilla pudding**, for a faux crème brûlée.

Equipment Grill or firc, skewers

APRICOTS WITH GOOEY NOUGAT

For 2 people

Cooked apricots turn divinely tender, sweet and sour. How can anyone not like them? Yet I live in a household where they are shunned, even by my children's friends. But I'm not giving up, because there's a small chance that you just might love them as much as I do.

4 apricots, halved and stoned
2 tablespoons of butter
1 tablespoon dark rum
2 pieces of nougat

Arrange the apricot halves on a piece of foil and make the sides of the foil into a boat. Dot the fruit with the butter, drizzle with the rum, then place a sliver of nougat in each apricot half. Cook on a covered grill for 10–15 minutes, until the fruit and nougat are softened.

Equipment Grill, foil

PIRATE BANANAS

For 4 people

A classic, and understandably so.

Grill 4 **bananas**, skin on, on a grill for about 5 minutes on each side until blackened and softened. Transfer them to a large plate or a board, cut them open down the middle and pop a few squares of **milk or dark chocolate** into the center of each one. Set aside for a few minutes for the chocolate to melt, then gently open up the bananas.

The Adult Version
A little **dark rum or whisky** drizzled on top, which you can warm and ignite first if desired.

The Child Version
A dollop of whipped cream or a blast of Reddi-Wip (great stuff when camping) down the center.

Equipment Grill

CRÊPES SUZETTE

For 4 people

Dedicated to my late father-in-law, Tony Bell, a great showman who as far as I know never cooked a meal in his life, like so many men of his generation. But he would take center stage at dinner parties, my poor mother-in-law having toiled all afternoon making delicate, fine crêpes that he would then finish with a flourish on a portable gas ring with copious amounts of flaming brandy.

Simmer 1 mug of **fresh orange juice** (blood orange if you can find it), 1 tablespoon of **sugar** and a few of tablespoons of **unsalted butter** in a pan

until reduced by about half. Add 4 **crêpes** (or 3 if they are especially large), folded in quarters, to the pan one by one and coat them in the syrup. Once they are warmed through, you can flambé them with **dark rum or brandy** for the full-on treat. Warm it over a flame in a tablespoon or small ladle, ignite and carefully pour it over the top.

Equipment Stove, pan

GRILLED MALLOMARS

Mallomars provide us with an instant S'more, a marshmallow covered in chocolate with a cookie underneath. Skewer these and grill briefly, held over a grill or in a fire, until the chocolate appears covered with beads of moisture, by which time the marshmallow will be deliciously mousse-like inside.

Equipment Grill or fire, skewers

S'MORES

The do-it-yourself campfire classic – skewer and grill **marshmallows**, slip them on to a small piece of **graham cracker**. Top with a couple of squares of **chocolate** and sandwich with a second cracker.

Equipment Grill or fire, skewers

PEACH CRUMBLE

For 6 people

A shortcut of a topping, one that produces an instant crumble. You could also scatter a few pieces of fudge, thinly sliced, over the top. There's no need to lug a special dish along with you for this dessert – improvize with something on hand. I find the Trangia frying pan does a great job of doubling up as a pie plate.

3–4 ripe peaches (ideally white), pitted and sliced
2 tablespoons squeezable honey
4 oatmeal pancakes (see page 69), crumbled

Scatter the peach slices over the bottom of a shallow pan that will hold the peaches in a crowded single layer. Drizzle with the honey, cover with foil and bake on the grid of a covered grill for about 10 minutes, until the fruit has softened and is sitting in lots of juice. Scatter the crumbled pancakes over the top and cook for another 5–10 minutes, again in a covered grill but without the foil. Good hot or cold.

Equipment Grill, pan, foil

SUMMER PUDDING FOR CAMPERS

For 4 people

This deconstructed summer pudding will work with any selection of berries. So it's great for all those blackberries you've arduously gathered. As always, heavenly with fresh whipped cream, a farmhouse treat should you be fortunate enough to find if camping in dairy country.

2 mugs of mixed berries (raspberries, blueberries, blackberries, etc.)
3 tablespoons sugar
4 small slices of day-old white bread

Gently heat the berries with the sugar in a small covered saucepan for about 10 minutes until they are sitting in lots of juice, stirring halfway through. Leave these to cool. Lay a slice of bread on each of 4 plates, ladle the fruit and juice over the top and leave to soak in for 10 minutes.

Equipment Stove, saucepan

OFF TO BED

Hunkering down for the night is no doubt aided by a steaming hot cup of cocoa, perhaps with the dash of dark rum for yours, and a delicious cookie. The easy route is one of those instant high-end hot chocolates, where all you need to do is pour hot milk or water over the mix. But there is nothing quite as delicious as properly made hot chocolate, sipped with hands wrapped snuggly around a mug, sitting at the entrance of your tent as the light is finally fading. Although I suspect there is an entire generation emerging who has no idea how to make it, given how convenient the mixes can be. If you are prepared to wash the pan, cocoa from scratch wins hands-down.

MUG OF COCOA

For 1 person

The important thing with making cocoa is to cook it, otherwise it will taste powdery and raw. It also needs to be added to warm or hot liquid in order

to blend. Place 1 heaping teaspoon of **unsweetened cocoa powder** and 1½ teaspoons of **sugar** in a small saucepan, and add a few table-spoons of **milk**. Gently heat until the milk is warm, then incorporate the cocoa powder using the back of a spoon. Add ½ a mug of milk and bring to a rolling boil.

Equipment Stove, saucepan

REAL CHOCOLATE HOT CHOCOLATE

For 1 person

Another route that saves on having to take a tub of cocoa powder with you is to pour ½ a mug of **boiling**

milk over a row of **dark chocolate squares** in a mug or bowl – breaking them into small pieces first. Leave it for a few minutes, then stir vigorously to melt. Sweeten to taste, and you could throw in a few **mini marshmallows** if you feel you haven't had your fill around the campfire.

AND YOURS? I was going to suggest a couple of teaspoons of **rum** splashed in, but depending on the circumstances that may seem a little conservative and a flatout nightcap might be in order. **Whisky** is another good camping companion – in the interest of an uninterrupted night's sleep you can consider it medicinal.

Equipment Stove, saucepan

BEST COOKIES FOR DUNKING

Shortbread Cookies
LU Petit Ecolier Biscuits
Graham Crackers
Ginger Snaps

All of which go very well with rum and whisky too.

RESOURCES

We recommend the following websites for campers:

www.worldspice.com
World Spice Merchants provide an online doorway to spices and blends from around the world, including those used in this book.

www.weber.com
Maker of iconic kettle grills. The "Smokey Joe" Gold is the travel size, or their domed "Weber Q" series and their "Go-Anywhere," shaped like a box, work on the same principles. You can also obtain chimney starters and extra-long tongs here.

www.cobbamerica.com
These now familiar, domed portable grills offer an eco-friendly solution to cooking whole chickens, as well as smaller cuts. They come with a convenient travel case. Accessories can be obtained from the website.

www.REI.com
A favorite one-stop camping resource, they provide an incredibly wide array of products including tents, sleeping bags, first aid supplies and everything for your camp kitchen. They can also be trusted for their range of stoves including Cobb, Coleman and Trangia.

www.bedbathandbeyond.com
This company is known for their expansive selection of home goods and cooking equipment. They stock a great deal of the everyday equipment recommended in this book including Lock & Lock storage containers.

www.campmor.com
This company carries camping supplies of all types including a nice selection of enamel tableware and a wide range of large (group) water carriers.

www.josephjoseph.com
This innovative kitchenware company has big, brightly-colored, lightweight solutions that are great for camping. Their magnetic measuring spoon has both teaspoon and tablespoon measures. Their stackable bowls come with a colander, a sieve and a lemon squeezer, and double as serving and cooking bowls. Their folding wooden cutting board is another great design.

www.preserveproducts.com
This eco-friendly company produces table and kitchenware made of 100% recycled #5 plastic. Their products are heavy-duty, reusable and can in turn be recycled. Lightweight and inexpensive, their products are great for an outdoor kitchen.

www.greenfeet.com
Coined "The Plant's Homestore®", this environmentally-conscious online store offers a wide range of lightweight bamboo and cork products.

www.specialtybottle.com
Providing the beauty and food industry with all types of storage options including travel-size tin and plastic jars and screwtop bottles, perfect for decanting small quantities of seasonings.

www.cheftools.com
This online supplier of professional equipment is fantastic when shopping for any specialty tool or gadget. Their selection of knives is large and they offer convenient traveling knife rolls for storage.

www.oxo.com
The now old-fashioned vegetable choppers with a blade that you push up and down have been all but replaced by food processors at home, but they still have a place in our "batterie de cuisine" on field trips.

www.lodgemfg.com
The cast-iron foundry Lodge produces classic cookware. Here you will find Dutch ovens in various sizes, tripods and lid lifters, for cooking one-pot dishes in true cowboy style over an open fire.

www.dreampot.com.au
This portable slow cooker contains two saucepans. Cook casseroles or one-pot dishes in about a quarter of their normal time, pop them into the insulated "Dream-Pot" and after a couple of hours you have a piping hot dish ready to serve.

www.green-pan.com
Greenpan lead the way in eco-friendly cooking technology. Their Thermolon™ coated pans are as light as non-stick aluminium and cook like a dream.

www.campingcomfortably.com
Enamelware mugs, plates and bowls are core camping equipment. They get better and better with wear and tear, stack and pack into nothing, and are unbreakable.

www.chefsresource.com
If like me you cannot live without a proper peppermill, even when camping, then look no further than Peugeot's miniature "Bistro" mill.

www.cathkidstonusa.com
Cath's aprons and tea towels are guaranteed to provide a home-making touch in any camping situation and make the gloomiest of days seem sunny and bright.

www.soulpad.com
This company specializes in traditional canvas bell-tents, that lend themselves to glamorous bohemian living, and are roomy enough to stand up in.

outdoorrugsonly.com
Regardless of whether you plan on picnicking, a plastic rug is bound to come in handy, whether it's to ward off the dew at breakfastime, or to sit on the ground after a rainshower. Mad Mats produce a rainbow of colorful and stylish designs.

www.thermos.com
Thermos Work Series steel flasks are a classic piece of design, that are guaranteed to keep fluids hot or cold for 24 hours.

www.amazon.com
When in doubt, this retail giant can find what you are looking for.

ACKNOWLEDGMENTS

Writing this book was spontaneous and last-minute, and led to a summer of fun lived out of doors, that wouldn't have been possible without many other people who entered into the spirit and made it all happen.

So with many thanks to:

Kyle Cathie and Judith Hannam, Senior Commissioning Editor, for giving us the opportunity. Lizzy Kremer, my agent at David Higham Associates, whose enthusiasm for camping fuelled the seed of an idea in the first place. Vicky Orchard, Editor, for her endless calm and efficiency. Annie Lee for her eagle eye in copy editing. Georgia Vaux for her splendid design of the book. Salima Hirani, for proofreading the manuscript. Isobel McLean, for her index. Julia Barder, as Sales and Marketing Director. Victoria Scales, for publicity. Jonnie Bell, for picking up a camera after so many years, and snapping away all summer. Louis Bell, our son, Benjamin Goodstein, and Will and Minna Moon White, campers supreme, also Gabi Tubbs. The Beards – Alex, Kate, Betty and Alfie, who thought they were coming to stay for a break. The Boxers – Kate and Charlie, who thought we were coming to stay for a break.

INDEX